Ye Are Free to Choose

Ye Are Free to Choose

Agency and the Latter-day Saint Woman

Edited by Maren M. Mouritsen

Brigham Young University

ISBN 0-8425-1964-5
Copyright 1981 Brigham Young University Publications. All rights reserved
Brigham Young University Press, Provo, Utah 84602
Printed in the United States of America
81 54176

Contents

Preface   vii

Ye Are Free to Choose   1
   Jeffrey R. Holland

The Rewards of Correct Choice   10
   Camilla E. Kimball

Decisions Determine Our Destiny   19
   Hugh W. Pinnock

Choices in a Nation of Alternatives   32
   Paula Hawkins

To Love Our God   41
   Lynn A. McKinlay

Pornography, Romance, and the Paradox of Freedom   50
   Marilyn Arnold

Pure Hearts and Pure Homes   63
   Patricia T. Holland

Sight and Insight: Mormon Women and Poetry   71
   Elouise Bell
   Sally H. Barlow
   Carol Lynn Pearson
   Vernice Wineera Pere

Unrighteous Dominion: A Panel Discussion   82
   Adrian P. Vanmondfrans, Moderator
   Brent Barlow
   B. Kent Harrison
   Carl S. Hawkins
   Grethe Ballif Peterson

Talents Bring Joy   98
   Lee Provancha Day

Fortifying Ourselves Against Evil   102
   Carol Ann Hawley

Freedom to Become 105
Mary Frances Sturlaugson

Preface

In the beginning, there was choice. In fact, from what we know of the earliest councils in Heaven, as chronicled in the scriptures, it seems that the issue of choice is one that has dominated human experiences from even before "the beginning." The theology of the Latter-day Saints is replete with examples of choices—good and bad, righteous and unrighteous, tentative and sure, eternal and very earthbound. It could even be postulated that much of what is recorded in the scriptures is, in the final analysis, a description of the process of choosing.

The right to choose was, after all, at the core of the struggle between Lucifer and Jesus. In the end, the right and, more especially, the responsibility to choose were at the heart of our Lord's *choice* to become the Savior through the Crucifixion and the Atonement. In a very real sense, he went to the Garden and died on the cross to preserve and to provide for each of us in our own ways the opportunity for choice.

This volume is a compilation of selected remarks pesented at the Sixth Annual Women's Conference held in February 1981 at Brigham Young University. After determining the theme, "Ye Are Free to Choose," its planners deliberately selected a diverse group of speakers whose choices have resulted in highly individual and unique life circumstances, yet whose lives reflect a oneness borne of shared faith. These speakers were asked specifically to consider personally and collectively their uniqueness, their own personal choices, and their reflections upon the principle of choice.

The keynote addresses given by Jeffrey R. Holland, Camilla Eyring Kimball, Hugh W. Pinnock, and Senator Paula Hawkins were delivered to the conference en masse at the beginning of each day and at the close of the conference. In addition, three well received presentations by Lynn McKinlay, Marilyn Arnold, and Patricia T. Holland have been included.

The second section of this volume contains a selection of poetry which is representative of the works of members of the panel that discussed the topic, "Do Good Mormons Make Bad Poets." Elouise Bell, the panel's moderator, provides a short introduction to the poetry itself and to the nature of poetry in general.

The format for the "Unrighteous Dominion" panel was less formal than that of some of the other workshops as the panel participants not only responded to questions from but engaged in a dialogue with the audience.

In editing this discussion, we have attempted to preserve the flavor of that session and to keep the responses of the panel members intact.

The panel, "Mormon Women: A Continuing Response to the World," grew out of our efforts at last year's conference to select several Mormon women who represented a wide diversity in their personal experiences, yet a unity in their commitment to the gospel. This year's panel was selected in that tradition—the tradition of making known our vast individual differences while affirming our unity, even in the struggle of choice in personal experiences. Three representatives of the seven panelists have been selected for inclusion here: a young, involved student; a young mother and brilliant ballerina; and the first black sister called into the mission field after the revelation on the extension of the priesthood blessings to all worthy members of the Church.

As you ponder the material each of these individuals chose to share, I invite you to reflect upon the context of choice and its many meanings. These are not stereotypical, one dimensional men and women; rather they are different, unique individuals who are still struggling, still choosing, and who see the world—and their ways of being in it—in very challenging and different ways. You will observe how choice permits, indeed, even invites, great diversity as we all work toward similar goals and ideals.

While it would be ideal to include herein each presentation given at the conference, the number of addresses delivered precludes our doing so; and the choices that had to be made were not easy ones. I am indebted not only to those whose works are included in this volume but to the many other speakers who gave willingly of their time and talent.

There is, of course, the tremendous debt that is owed to those individuals who worked behind the scenes, contributing so unselfishly to the success of the conference and to the production of this work, for whom the only reward is the joy of working together in an effort to which we were all so deeply committed.

Administrators of Brigham Young University provide a supportive environment for this type of creative educational endeavor. President Jeffrey R. Holland was at the forefront, not only as the opening keynote speaker, but throughout the year of planning, as were Dean David M. Sorenson and Dr. Carolyn J. Rasmus. The executive council of the Associated Students of Brigham Young University supplied not only financial support for the endeavor, but also fine leadership.

The conference chairwoman, Rose Oliver, along with those members of her steering committee and subcommittees, worked countless hours in planning and carrying out the myriad details inherent in such a massive effort. Tamara M. Quick and Ardeth G. Kapp provided not only excellent advisement to Rose and her colleagues but provided valuable and creative insights into the planning of the conference.

Finally, the actual editing and production of this work was handled most professionally and cordially by James P. Bell of the BYU Press. And Kimberly Ford provided valuable assistance in bringing together the many pieces that now comprise this work.

To each and every one who contributed to the conference and to this volume is owed a debt that will be paid in full only when you, the reader, find not only reward but pleasure in this volume. It is our sincere hope that such will, indeed, be the case.

Maren M. Mouritsen

Ye Are Free to Choose

Jeffrey R. Holland

Dr. Jeffrey R. Holland was inaugurated in the fall of 1980 as the ninth president of Brigham Young University. His appointment follows a distinguished teaching and administrative career within the Church's educational system, which included a four-year term as commissioner. President Holland is an alumnus of BYU, having received his bachelor's degree with highest honors and his master's degree with distinction. A Yale University Fellow, he received a Ph.D. from that institution.

In addition to his formal teaching and administrative career, President Holland has served in leadership positions in a number of local and national church, educational, and civic organizations.

He and his wife, the former Patricia Terry, are the parents of three children.

On behalf of the Trustees and administration of Brigham Young University, we welcome you to this campus and these activities. For Latter-day Saints everywhere, including those who are not able to enroll here as matriculated students, BYU is your university. You are always welcome here.

We specifically welcome you to our sixth annual Women's Conference. The theme for this conference is taken from the tenth chapter of 2 Nephi, verse 23. Similar expressions are found elsewhere in our scriptures. It is my distinct honor to be invited to say a word or two about that theme, which I shall try to do in just a moment. But before getting to that, may I make a brief preface to the idea of the conference itself—what it is and, just as importantly, what it is not.

As many of you know, I am new to BYU, at least in this present assignment. Undoubtedly that is the only reason I have been invited to greet you. I assume it is part of a year-long rite of passage. In any case I come to this conference knowing that five other similar events and much contemporary history both in and out of the Church have gone before. Such a circumstance reminds me of something President J. Reuben Clark, speaking on this campus in 1938, said of the great Webster-Hayne debate that had raged in the Senate in the 1830s over the Foot Resolution. The Foot Resolution dealt with the use of public lands in the emerging new nation, and the debate over it developed into a magnificent consideration of great constitutional issues in the law. After that war of words had been storming along for weeks, the senator from Massachusetts stopped nearly in midsentence and said in his inimitable way to the presiding officer:

> Mr. President: When the mariner has been tossed for many days in thick weather, and on an unknown sea, he naturally avails himself at the first pause in the storm, the earliest glance of the sun, to take his latitude, and ascertain how far the elements have driven him from his true course. Let me imitate this prudence, and, before we float farther on the waves of this debate, refer to the point from which we departed, that we may at least be able to conjecture where we now are. [Mr. President] I ask for a reading of the resolution.

That is a very eloquent and Websterian way of saying, "After all this time I need just a brief reminder as to what it is we are talking about." Because I won't be able to round you all up at the end of the conference, I propose to "read the resolution" now, at the beginning, while we are still safely in port. It may help us put not only these next three days but also five earlier conferences and much contemporary history into some context.

First, as to what this conference is *not*.

Resolved: This is *not* a sub-rosa session of a general Relief Society conference, nor a surreptitious gathering of Young Women's presidencies. Indeed this is not an attempt to supplement (which is not their wish) nor supplant (which is not our wish) *any* auxiliary activity of the Church. We do the University, the General Authorities, and the officers of those auxiliaries a disservice if that impression is given. This conference is what it is: an activity of the Associated Women Students of BYU to which any others willing to keep our standards—male or female, member or nonmember—are welcome, which is the rule for virtually all campus activities. Indeed this is but one of some six hundred special workshops and conferences to be held at BYU this year. A university is, by definition, in that kind of business. We are genuinely thrilled at your attendance, but in fairness to Presidents Barbara Smith and Elaine Cannon, if we see in the bowling alley any clandestine meeting of cultural refinement teachers or the furtive glance and passing of notes from one Laurel leader to another, we are going to tear up your Cougar Eat meal tickets. With that settled, welcome to the University.

So much for what the conference is not. Now just a resolution or two, considerably more serious, as to the premises on which the conference has been organized. (And these brief comments will lead me into the theme that has been chosen.) It is probably important to say now what will immediately become obvious—that I will not be speaking about women and women's concerns per se. I will, rather, be speaking about choices which women—and men—have to make. In fact, let me go one step farther—farther back that is. I am not really even going to speak of choices but rather of the theology of choice, which theology undergirds and overarches every choice we make. If there is a *key* note to this conference, it seems to me that this theology provides it. I leave to others the specific applications to women in the 1980s that these three days together will provide.

With that I continue an introductory reading of the resolution.

Resolved: That God is our Father, that we are his children, and that he loves us deeply and equally. Indeed he "is no respecter of persons" in terms of his divine care and protection, nor in demanding individual obedience to the laws of heaven. We are in this world as brothers and sisters with common purposes and uncommon promises.

Resolved: That as children we are very different, not only woman to man but also man to man and woman to woman. Indeed our individuality speaks of a personality, an intelligence if you will, that was never created or made and that has always been independent in that sphere in which God has placed it. That unique personality—yours and mine—has developed admirably for the most part, but it is still only a type and a shadow of what it can and should become as it obeys those laws and pursues those promises.

Resolved: That we do a monumental injustice to ourselves and to heaven if we see *priesthood* as merely a twentieth-century buzzword synonymous with "men" or "male administration." The priesthood is *not* a human being, though human beings—male and female—are served by it. The priesthood is, according to the Prophet Joseph Smith, the

> channel through which all knowledge, doctrine, ... and every important matter is revealed from heaven. [Indeed its institution was] prior to the foundation of this earth, ... and is the channel through which the Almighty commenced revealing His glory at the beginning ... and through which He has continued to reveal Himself ... to the present time, and through which He will make known His purposes to the end of time. [*Teachings of the Prophet Joseph Smith,* comp. Joseph Fielding Smith (Salt Lake City: Deseret Book Co., 1938), p. 167]

In short the priesthood can exist without the Church, but the Church cannot exist without the priesthood.

Further resolved: That through the priesthood *both* men and women enjoy the saving ordinances of God, including those of the holy temple. Furthermore they find in that priesthood the power of godliness in time and in eternity, power by which *both* women and men can see the face of God and live. Indeed without priesthood protection and the transcendent influence of our covenants we would, according to Moses, wither and die in God's presence.

Resolved: That Jesus is the Only Begotten Son of God, Alpha and Omega, the Great I Am. His presence provides the brackets to our existence. His is the one life held up as a light in a dark place, and it is by that light that we grope toward glory. He is the ideal by which both men and women must measure their mortal efforts. His divine attributes and characteristics have sometimes been described as "masculine" (such as his courage and his strength) and sometimes as "feminine" (such as his sorrow and his compassion). Those are, of course, neither masculine nor feminine attributes but rather Christian attributes. Or, better yet, when seen in him, holy attributes.

Resolved: That Joseph Smith, the Vermont schoolboy; Spencer W. Kimball, the twentieth-century Job; and all their associates in between were and are prophets of God. They are the very oracles of heaven in our dispensation, rightful successors to the throne of Moses. And when God speaks on doctrine, it will be to them. We have been promised that God would take them rather than let us be led astray. Their selfless, sacrificing devotion is a matter of public record, and their blessing to us is inestimable. "We thank thee, O God, for a prophet."

Now I return to 2 Nephi 10:23. As I warned you, this is school, not Church. I'm going to give you a pop quiz. Your entire grade depends on this one quiz. Are you ready?

Question: "Over what issue or proposition was the War in Heaven fought?"

That is the whole exam. How did you do?

Now I won't ask for a show of hands, but everyone who said "free agency" or something like it—and I assume that is virtually everyone—has failed the exam. That is *not* the right answer. I gave you a one-question exam. Your whole future depended on it. Eternity was weighing in the balance. You've gone down the tube.

Now before you slip out to the phone booth, call Salt Lake, and have me working for the Methodists tomorrow, let me explain why free agency is not the right answer to that question. It isn't that it's wrong; it's just that it is not completely right. As I understand it, free agency was not the *original* issue over which the great War in Heaven was fought, regardless of what Sister Brown told you when you were a Merrie Miss. Certainly it did *become* an issue. That's why we have it as a theme today. That's why the scriptures are laden with the language. I am not denying the fact that it *became* part of the issue. I am just suggesting that some other proposition came earlier.

Now that I have made you sufficiently uneasy, I will ask the question again: If it is not free agency, then what was the issue over which the great premortal battle was fought?

May I suggest an answer? It was presented when God himself, our Eternal Father (and for all I know our Eternal Mother stood with him, though I know nothing of that and we have nothing in the record) said to you and to me and to all others in our family, "Do you want to be as we are?" I think that question started the War in Heaven. The issue was—and is—godhood. Now incidental to that and almost instantly on the heels of it comes an issue like having free agency. You can't be exalted without exercising free agency. But when the discussion first began, I think the question from our heavenly parents was, "Do you want to be as we are? Do you want to become gods and goddesses, kings and queens, priests and priestesses?"

It was at that point that I believe Satan rose up to say, "I am unalterably opposed to that proposition." I do not know whether he used those words. He may have been more skillful than that, but I believe that is what he felt then and feels now. That is when the battle lines began to be drawn, and we started to divide, in some spiritual way, contending for the loyalties of men and women, our own brothers and sisters, in that great premortal council. It seems to me that if you examine carefully the scriptures and if, in fact, you look closely at our daily lives, you will find that Satan was saying then and is saying now that he does not want any of us to become like God.

And so he proposed an alternative plan to his father's by saying, in effect, "I will provide an option for these people that will guarantee not one single soul will become a god or a goddess, or a king or a queen, or a priest or a priestess. Why? Because I want to be god, and I want to be the only god." As I paraphrase from the fourth chapter of Moses, Satan said in effect, "I want the honor and the power and the glory and the privilege and the priesthood. And I want it all. There isn't any room for anyone at the top but me."

From that day to this, in his overweening, self-centered, egotistical, demeaning, demanding way, Satan has opposed your eternal possibilities. His opposition to free agency, to the family, to priesthood powers, to anything that provides you with the keys, principles, and truths that enable you to return to the presence of God and indeed be like him, is designed to keep you from doing so.

We may not remember the details, but the nature of the conflict and the conditions placed on our having a chance to come to earth and to keep our second estate indicate that we wanted the chance to grow and become. We were willing to take the risks. We were willing to face the pain, the poverty, the heartache, and some of the disappointments. We were certainly willing to accept blessings, revelation, the realization of eternal promises, and the opportunity to see God's heavenly countenance once again. We were somehow able to summon the courage, knowing what we knew, to act on our knowledge that our real chance, our real possibility, would come through the Father's plan, ratified by his Only Begotten Son and in turn by all of us, but opposed, even in that setting, by Satan and a third of the great heavenly family.

If I say nothing else of value to you on this day, it is very important to me that you do not see choice as an end in itself. That would be a disservice to this conference, and to what we believe as expressed in the tenth chapter of 2 Nephi. Furthermore, it would be a disservice to everything that I think we stand for in the Church. I am not particularly interested in or impressed by choice for choice's sake. I am immensely impressed by and deeply devoted to choices that are made in the context of the question, "Will this enable me to become as God is?" When made in that light, our choices determine our future. I'm not nearly as interested in conferences about cultural choices or social choices or political choices or temporal choices. But to talk of eternal choices, about the consequence of heavenly opportunity, about unlimited capacity, about whatever it is that opens the windows of eternity and the powers of priesthood that antedate you and me, then I am deeply interested.

Now, if godhood was the fundamental issue around which other issues then began to move, and I believe with all my heart that it was, I ask you to go with me to this board as I take this idea one step further. We are going to leave behind the premortal conflict and go to the Garden of Eden where the issue very quickly became one of whether to stay or leave. That was the issue then, and that is the issue now. You will recall that Adam and Eve left, and all of you know why. But I would like to ask that you divorce yourself for a moment from all the things you know or assume about the reasons they left and suppose for a moment they had said, "Let's stay."

Why would Adam and Eve want to stay? Was there anything attractive about Eden? Well, for one thing, they would be with Heavenly Father. If we are going to talk about the reasons for staying in the Garden, one is remaining in the presence of God, walking and talking in the cool of the evening with a Heavenly Father. That is not our lot now. I am not minimizing prayer, or inspiration, or special spiritual opportunities, but these are not quite the same as walking and talking in the Garden with God the Eternal Father. Another reason for remaining would be the abundance and plenty, the absence of thorns, thistles, and noxious weeds. What about the human experiences? Would there be conflict or pain or disease or death or dissatisfaction or a tough economy? There would be none of those things. In fact, this was a very, very attractive place; it was paradise. In fact, our tenth Article of Faith states that during the Millennium, the earth will be renewed to its paradisiacal glory, to a condition similar to the Garden of Eden. We long for that day, and we believe it will come.

Now, with all these reasons to stay, there must have been some reason to go, or Adam and Eve wouldn't have, and we wouldn't have agreed to their decision and applauded it. But the list of reasons to leave is very short; in fact, all of the earlier pluses became minuses when Adam and Eve left the Garden. They would no longer be able to walk and talk with God, although they could establish a relationship with him. They would no longer enjoy the abundance found in the Garden but would, instead, have to cope with thorns, thistles, and noxious weeds, earning their bread by the sweat of their brows. They would have to face sickness and sorrow and pain and ultimately death. And all of these minuses were passed on to Adam and Eve's children—you and me.

Given all these problems, why did Adam and Eve leave the Garden, and why were we so happy when they did? What were Adam and Eve unable to have in the garden?

One thing they could not have was children. Father Lehi told his son Jacob:

> If Adam had not transgressed he would not have fallen, but he would have remained in the Garden of Eden. And all things which were created must have remained in the same state in which they were after they were created; and they must have remained forever, and

had no end.
And they would have had no children. [2 Nephi 2:22-23]

Now, I don't know why they wouldn't have children; the scriptures just say they wouldn't if they had remained in the Garden.

How did Lehi know to teach that to Jacob? One obvious way is that it could have been revealed to him. He was giving a patriarchal blessing, and he was entitled to that inspiration. The priesthood is the power by which such truths are communicated. But there is another way he could have learned it, and this is important in the context of this conference. He could have learned it through reading the brass plates of Laban, which Lehi and his family had in their possession. He could have read in the brass plates—just as we read in the fifth chapter of Moses verse 11—"And Eve, his wife, heard all these things and was glad, saying: Were it not for our transgression we never should have had seed." And with that knowledge they made their choice to leave and then later reaffirmed that it never would have been otherwise.

What is the other thing offered only outside the Garden? It is revealed in the one true thing that Satan said to Eve. In a whole fistful of lies he said one true thing. As he pointed to a certain tree in the garden, Eve told him that she could not eat of the fruit of that particular tree because she would die. And Satan replied, "Ye shall not surely die [that's a lie, which is typical of him], . . . [but] ye shall become as gods, knowing good and evil." [which was the truth, very untypical of him]." (See Moses 4:8-11.)

That is all I know about choices. And that is what your conference is about. It is about growth and development and possibility and progress. It is about eternal progression and beginning to do something about it, which is why we have a university and why we say that women—as well as men—are supposed to be educated. It is why we talk about potential and growth and purity and perfection and extension and expansion. And do you think Satan would not be opposed to such goals and to anything that would assist a person in achieving these goals? How long does it take him to strike the human family, especially one that is gospel-centered and of an eternal nature? Not long. He strikes instantly. Have you noticed that both the Bible and the Book of Mormon begin with Satan attempting to destroy a family? In light of the eternal potential women have, if they make the proper choices, do you think that Satan might have anything to do with the present controversies over women's issues, over discrimination against them, or with their disappointments or their discouragements?

Now, I need to have a young woman come up here for a moment. Would you [pointing to the first row] come up, please?
What is your name?
Mary.
You are pretty young to be to this conference aren't you?
Yes.
Are you sloughing school?
Sort of.

Do your parents know you are here?
Yes.
Do you have any brothers?
Yes.
Do you have any sisters?
No.
You are the only girl in your family?
Yes.
The *only* girl?
Yes.
Are you proud to be a girl?
Yes.
Do you think your parents are proud you're a girl?
Yes.
Do you think your dad loves you?
Yes.
Do you think he wants every righteous thing in this world for you?
Yes.
Does he dream about you and pray about you and love you with all his heart?
Yes.
Who is your dad?
You are.

My friends, this is Mary Alice Holland. She is our only daughter. She is also the light of her dad's life. Do I dream about her and pray about her and love her with all my heart? No one who is not the father of a daughter will ever know how much I dream about her and pray about her and love her with all my heart.

Do I want her to be happy? Do I want her to grow? Do I want her to be, in righteousness, everything in time or eternity she possibly, humanly, divinely can be? What foolish questions! This is bone of my bone, flesh of my flesh! This is my only daughter! Of course I want it! Do I want her disappointed or disillusioned or discriminated against? I want her happy, fulfilled, and blossoming into all that God intended her to be and discussed with her a long time ago. I want her to have strong family bonds in time and eternity, and I want her to be a queen, a priestess unto the Most High.

The gospel of Jesus Christ gives her the *one* chance she has. Help her with her choices. She's eleven today. Tomorrow she is seventeen. The day after tomorrow she is gone away to start a life and family of her own. Then she is in your hands—you who will be her teachers, her guides, her friends. She already stands on the border of womanhood, that unique, mysterious sisterhood from which I and all other men are forever excluded. Soon she will fully be your sister. And she will always be my daughter.

Mary, you are free to choose. Ask—and pray—for at least two things. First, that you will work hard in your own behalf and equally hard in the behalf of others to become all that Heavenly Father wants you to become. Second, that you will never ever forget who it was who loved your life enough to give His own in order to set you free.

It is in his name that I testify of his gospel—even Jesus Christ. Amen.

The Rewards of Correct Choices

Camilla E. Kimball

Camilla Eyring Kimball, the first child of eight born to Caroline Romney and Edward C. Eyring, is the mother of four children and has been the wife of President Spencer W. Kimball for over fifty years. During that time she has utilized her formal training in home economics and has instilled in her family a love for learning of all kinds.

Sister Kimball attended the Brigham Young Academy where she received her teaching certificate. After teaching home economics at the Millard Academy in Hinckley, Utah, she attended the University of California at Berkeley and the Utah Agricultural College in Logan. She then took a position with the Gila Academy in Thatcher, Arizona.

An excellent role model for Church members throughout the world, Sister Kimball has been honored by both Brigham Young University and Ricks College as the recipient of their Exemplary Womanhood Awards.

I am pleased to meet with so many of you who are here to participate in this women's conference. It is a marvelous opportunity to exchange ideas, and it serves to remind us of the wide range of choices we make in life and the importance of choosing well.

It has been a circuitous path that brings me back to BYU again sixty-eight years after I first arrived here as a frightened seventeen-year-old refugee from the revolution in Mexico. That was a major step in the great lifelong adventure in education I have enjoyed, an adventure that continues today as much as ever. I have always reserved a special place in my heart for this school, though it bears scant resemblance today to the little academy I came to in 1912. I imagine that date sounds like pre-historic time to you young people.

Actually, I have lived from the days of the horse and buggy to the age of the jet plane. When I was a little girl we lived in the village of Colonia Juarez, Mexico. My grandmother Romney lived eighteen miles away in Colonia Dublan. Once a month the family made the trip so my mother could visit her mother.

There was one special trip we made in the buggy with a special team of horses papa had purchased. We boasted about making this trip in the unheard-of space of three hours. By contrast, just a few months ago my husband and I flew in a jet from New York City to London in three hours and twenty-nine minutes. That seems almost impossible.

The theme of this conference, as you have been reminded several times, is from the second book of Nephi. May I review with you its context.

Lehi and his fractious band had been led by God out of Palestine across the sea to a new land. Not many generations had been born when Jacob, ordained to be teacher of his people, delivered a great sermon in which he summarized the message of redemption he had been preaching for many years. One gets the impression that he was speaking to a somewhat discouraged people.

He reviewed at length the Lord's great covenants with the house of Israel, to which the Nephites belonged, and reminded them that in due time the Lord would take upon himself flesh and suffer and die for all men. He then concluded his teaching for the day and promised to continue the next day.

When the Nephites gathered again Jacob told them of an angelic visitation he had received during the night. In that revelation additional information was given him regarding the earthly ministry of the Christ, and he was told again that the land to which they had been led had been set aside as an inheritance for the peoples who had been led there. Jacob, in seeking to comfort this band of people cut off from their homeland, reminded them that the Lord was continually mindful of them in their exile and that wherever they might be and whatever their circumstances, their personal struggle for salvation must go on just the same. He said, "Therefore, cheer up your hearts, and remember that ye are free to act for yourselves—to choose the way of everlasting death or the way of eternal life.

"Wherefore, my beloved brethren, reconcile yourselves to the will of God, and not to the will of the devil and the flesh." (2 Ne. 10:23-24.) Nephi was highly selective in what portions of Jacob's sermon he recorded, so he must have considered this passage to be important. It states a fundamental principle of the gospel: that we are free to choose. We call this principle free will or free agency. I have thought about the concept of free agency, and it has seemed to me to have four components: first, the existence of alternatives; second, knowledge of those alternatives; third, the ability to choose from among the alternatives; and fourth, responsibility for the choice made.

First then, there must be alternatives or contrast or opposition. No passage of scripture is more explicit on this issue than Lehi's great discourse to his son Jacob:

> For it must needs be, that there is an opposition in all things. If not so, my first-born in the wilderness, righteousness could not be brought to pass, neither wickedness, neither holiness nor misery, neither good nor bad. Wherefore, all things must needs be a compound in one; wherefore, if it should be one body it must needs remain as dead, having no life neither death, nor corruption nor incorruption, happiness nor misery, neither sense nor insensibility.

> Wherefore, it must needs have been created for a thing of naught; wherefore there would have been no purpose in the end of its creation. Wherefore, this thing must needs destroy the wisdom of God and his eternal purposes, and also the power, and the mercy, and the justice of God. [2 Ne. 2:11-12]

John the Revelator expressed a similar divine disdain for blandness, quoting the Spirit as saying of the Church in Laodicea: "I know thy works, that thou art neither cold nor hot: I would thou wert cold or hot. So then because thou art lukewarm, and neither cold nor hot, I will spue thee out of my mouth." (Rev. 3:15-16.)

Freedom to choose presupposes the existence of alternatives. Change and contrast and opposition give vitality to life. Even sin and rebellion serve a function. The futility of existence without contrast, without sin, is underscored in Lehi's explanation of the Fall:

> If Adam had not transgressed . . . all things which were created must have remained in the same state in which they were after they were created; and they must have remained forever, and had no end.
>
> And they would have . . . remained in a state of innocence, having no joy, for they knew no misery; doing no good, for they knew no sin.
>
> But behold, all things have been done in the wisdom of him who knoweth all things.
>
> Adam fell that men might be; and men are, that they might have joy.
>
> And the Messiah cometh in the fulness of time, that he may redeem the children of men from the fall. And because that they are redeemed from the fall they become free forever, knowing good from evil; to act for themselves and not to be acted upon. . . . free to choose liberty and eternal life . . . or to choose captivity and death. [2 Ne. 2:22-27]

We have learned that when astronauts remain in space a long time they lose mineralization in their bones, and unless they guard against it, weightlessness can also affect their hearts and other muscles enough to make them unfit when they return to an environment where gravity exerts its constant pull. Likewise, we are inclined to long for ease in our lives, but it is a common observation that those who have struggled and overcome are the ones who have the greatest satisfaction.

The passage from the Revelation of John decrying lukewarmness continues in this vein: "I counsel thee to buy of me gold tried in the fire, that thou mayest be rich. . . .

"As many as I love, I rebuke and chasten; be zealous therefore, and repent. . . .

"He that hath an ear, let him hear." (Rev. 3:18-19, 22.)

If the first requisite of free agency is the existence of alternatives, the second is knowledge of those alternatives. If we are afloat on the sea, out of sight of land, and if there is one direction that will soonest bring us to safe harbor but we have no way of ascertaining that direction, we cannot fairly be judged good or bad sailors for picking whatever course chance gives us.

The scriptures remind us over and over again that without knowledge there is not full moral responsibility. Paul wrote, "For there is no respect of persons with God. For as many as have sinned without law shall also perish without law." (Rom. 2:12.)

And Jacob taught the Lehites:

> Where there is no law given there is no punishment; and where there is no punishment there is no condemnation; and where there is no condemnation the mercies of the Holy One of Israel have claim upon them, because . . . the atonement satisfieth the demands of his justice upon all those who have not the law given to them . . . and they are restored to that God who gave them breath. . . . But wo unto him that has . . . all the commandments of God, like unto us, and that transgresseth them, and that wasteth the days of his probation, for awful is his state. [2 Ne. 9:25-27]

The prime example of one who stands innocent because he lacks knowledge is the child. The rest of us will come sooner or later to knowledge. King Benjamin said: "The time shall come when the knowledge of a Savior shall spread throughout every nation. . . .

"And behold, when that time cometh, none shall be found blameless before God, except it be little children" (Mos. 3:21-22).

Awareness of alternatives is important, but sometimes it may be too much to speak of "knowledge." Often we must walk by faith, not discerning the choices clearly. "Good and evil," "black and white," and "right and wrong" are the simple cases, the extremes. Nearer the middle it is difficult to distinguish boundaries. If the light is dim, one should seek more light, but ultimately he must make his choices with whatever light he has received.

The third component of free agency is to choose from among the alternatives we know. Choice in life is not just an occasional thing. We are afloat on a sea of choices. And we ought not to think that we can avoid accountability by refusing to make a choice because refusing to decide is itself a choice—a choice to be borne wherever external forces will take us.

Choice has meaning only with reference to real alternatives. We are not wholly independent of circumstance; wind and tide and current all have their influence. We can choose the direction of our striving and head for whatever shore we wish, but we may be driven back like the Arctic explorer who struggled all day on pack ice toward the North Pole only to find that the current had moved him farther back than where he had started. We may wonder at strong forces that seem to overwhelm our poor powers of choice, but it is part of our faith that in matters of eternal importance our destiny is indeed in our hands.

Free agency does not mean that all possibilities are open to us. One cannot choose to be younger or more beautiful, to know what is unknowable, or to be successful or loved. A person can choose to do things that may tend to bring about some of those conditions, but his or her ultimate achievement is outside individual control. Happily, we understand, the judgment of God is to be based largely on what we have done with the choices open to us—not on absolute results, but on progress. We are responsible for direction and effort.

Once we understand the options actually open to us, it still takes courage to choose rightly. And sometimes we need to be reminded over and over again. Joshua, aging and seeing the children of Israel beginning to stray again after the strange gods of their neighbors, called his people together to elicit from them one last commitment before he died. First, he reminded them of how the Lord had fought their battles when they came to occupy the Promised Land. He said, speaking for God, "I have given you a land for which ye did not labour, and cities which ye built not, and ... vineyards ... which ye planted not." Joshua then challenged them: "Now therefore fear the Lord, and serve him in sincerity and in truth; and put away the gods which your fathers served.... Choose you this day whom ye will serve ... : but as for me and my house, we will serve the Lord."

The people responded, "Therefore will we also serve the Lord."

But Joshua prodded, "He will not forgive your transgressions ... if ye forsake the Lord, and serve strange gods."

The people said, "Nay; but we will serve the Lord."

And Joshua said, "Ye are witnesses against yourselves that ye have chosen you the Lord, to serve him."

And they replied, "We are witnesses."

Joshua said, "Now therefore put away ... the strange gods which are among you and incline your heart unto the Lord God of Israel."

The people chorused, "The Lord our God will we serve, and his voice will we obey." (See Josh. 24:13-24.)

You see how Joshua, in drawing out those audience responses, worked at getting his people to make a choice and then to repeat it and reaffirm it. He then set up a great stone as a memorial of their promise, to stand as a permanent witness to their covenant. And we should remember that gospel ordinances are designed to remind us again and again of our commitments.

Having to choose is every person's lot. Even those great and good spirits whom God chose in the premortal existence to be his rulers had to undergo the same testing process. Alma speaks of the high priests who were "called and prepared from the foundation of the world according to the foreknowledge of God, on account of their exceeding faith and good works," but he notes that they were "in the first place ... left to choose good or evil; therefore they having chosen good, and exercising exceeding great faith, are called with a holy calling." Others who "in the first place ... were on the same standing with their brethren ... might have had as great privilege" but they "reject the Spirit of God on account of the hardness of their hearts and blindness of their minds." (See Alma 13:1-4.)

Sometimes the results of our choices come promptly, but often outcomes are long delayed so that our "knowledge" is only tentative and is based upon what we are told by spokesmen we believe and upon extension of our past experience.

It is part of the Lord's plan that we see through the glass only darkly for the most part (1 Cor. 13:12), and that there be trial of our faith. The Lord said, through Brigham Young, "My people must be tried in all things, that they may be prepared to receive the glory that I have for them, even the glory of Zion; and he that will not bear chastisement is not worthy of my kingdom" (D&C 136:31). These factors make our choosing more difficult and stressful.

Sometimes we feel nearly overwhelmed and would like to deny responsibility for our decisions, but we are taught that we may not do so. Joseph Smith said that "the Devil has no power over us, only as we permit him" (*Teachings of the Prophet Joseph Smith,* comp. Joseph Fielding Smith [Salt Lake City: Deseret Book Co., 1938], p. 181). The same principle is expressed by Paul: "God ... will not suffer you to be tempted above that ye are able; but will with the temptation also make a way to escape, that ye may be able to bear it" (1 Cor. 10:13).

The final component of free agency is that we bear responsibility for our choices. Samuel the Lamanite said on this subject: "Remember, my brethren, that whosoever perisheth, perisheth unto himself, ... for behold, ye are ... permitted to act for yourselves; ... God hath given unto you knowledge and he hath made you free" (Hel. 14:30).

Once we make an understanding choice among alternatives, we have responsibility for each choice poorly made and can expect rich reward for each choice made wisely.

Our accountability is individual. As Ezekiel says, "the son shall not bear the iniquity of the father, neither shall the father bear the iniquity of the son: the righteousness of the righteous shall be upon him, and the wickedness of the wicked shall be upon him" (Ezek. 18:20). And it is not only the momentous decisions that we must account for: "Every idle word that men shall speak, they shall give account thereof in the day of judgment" (Matt. 12:36). As Alma said, "If we have hardened our hearts against the word ... our words will condemn us, yea, all our works will condemn us; ... and our thoughts will also condemn us" (Alma 12:13-14).

Rewards for correct choices come in all shapes and sizes, large and small, but none are insignificant. Blessings come by obedience: "When we obtain any blessing from God, it is by obedience to that law upon which it is predicated" (D&C 130:21).

If we avoid harmful drugs and eat wholesome foods, we are promised improved health, hidden treasures of knowledge, stamina, and protection from the destroying angel. (See D&C 89.)

If we bring our tithes and offerings into the Lord's storehouse, he will open the windows of heaven to pour out overflowing blessings; he will protect our crops and will make our land delightsome. (See Mal. 3:8-10.)

If we keep a personal journal, we can expect to be held in honorable memory by our descendants, who will learn from our experiences and testimony.

If we love one another, Christ will love us. If we are his disciples, he will call us his friends. (See John 15:10-14.)

If we observe the Lord's day, confessing, fasting, and praying, and doing so cheerfully, the fullness of the earth is ours. (See D&C 59:16.)

If we render service to one another, trying to repay our Father, we can never catch up because he will shower us with more blessings. (See Mos. 2.)

In a hundred other ways our choice to obey the Lord will help us reap a rich reward.

There is one reward, above all else, we may hope for. That is exaltation. The Lord gives us the free gift of resurrection, even if we have made wrong choices, but we can partake fully of his atoning sacrifice only if we meet his conditions. The passage from which our theme is taken admonishes us to "reconcile yourselves to the will of God ... and remember ... that it is only in and through the grace of God that ye are saved. Wherefore, may God raise you from death by the power of the resurrection, and also from everlasting death by the power of the atonement, that ye may be received into the eternal kingdom of God, that ye may praise him through grace divine." (2 Ne. 10:24-25.) We are told further that if we make the eternal marriage covenant through the priesthood power and abide in that covenant, then we shall pass to exaltation and glory and a continuation of the seeds forever and be gods from everlasting to everlasting, joining Abraham, Isaac, and Jacob in that blessed condition. (See D&C 132:19-20, 37.)

Many of the rewards, however certain, are far in the future. It requires faith to endure to the end when the rewards seem so long delayed. It is as with the Lord's coming: some will give up in despair; others will still be prepared, their lamps having been filled with oil.

When he came the first time, many had given up their faith that the sign Samuel the Lamanite had predicted would mark Christ's birth would actually occur. They thought the time was past. But the faithful, despite threats of imminent death, remained steadfast, knowing in whom they trusted.

In an ultimate sense, of course, we cannot earn salvation by our wise choices or our good deeds. We do what we can, but the goal is far beyond us. Someone else must bridge the chasm, "for we know that it is by grace that we are saved, after all we can do" (2 Ne. 25:23).

Jesus reminded his disciples, "Ye have not chosen me, but I have chosen you" (John 15:16). We seek to follow the Savior, adhering to his teachings, emulating his virtues, enduring whatever burdens may be placed upon us, bearing his name, accepting his great sacrifice, and calling upon his grace. We then have hope that he will reach out and draw us to him, making us more than we have made ourselves.

I have tried to take you with me through my reading and thinking about this great principle of the gospel to the idea that we are both free and responsible. On the one hand, it helps me to be more diligent if I can see my place in the larger scheme of things and if I can be reminded what glorious things await us. But on the other hand, there is often so great a gap between our hope of heaven and the daily round of mundane activities that I must struggle to keep them in eternal perspective. I learn great principles best in simple applications.

I can see clearly that my earthly life has been greatly affected by choices I have made along the way. My choice of friends has helped keep me straight. I have had friends who expected me to be good, and I have tried not to disappoint them.

My choice to obey my parents had the same effect. I recall my first real date to a dance. I had accepted the invitation from a boy before I talked to my parents. My father objected to the boy. My tears got me permission to go with him just that once, but I did not go with him again; I did not consider disobeying my father. Though I did not always understand or agree with his judgment, I knew he had my welfare at heart. Several years later, when I began going with Spencer Kimball, my father had no objection. He recognized him as a man of quality.

It is obvious how much the direction of my life has been affected by my choice of a husband. On the eve of our wedding I shed a great many tears over the uncertainty caused by the prospect of his having to go off to war, over giving up the plans I had made for a profession, and over the magnitude of the commitment I was making. But I knew that he was a faithful, energetic, capable person and that I loved him very much. I believed that together we could have a happy life and move step by step toward returning, with our family, to our Father in Heaven. Choosing that road has made all the difference.

My decision to pursue an education and become a teacher gave me some skills I could put to use in the family and in the Church and community. Because I chose to read for pleasure I ended up with an activity which has enriched my life greatly and has helped me motivate my children to love learning. For some time I was the volunteer librarian in our small-town library in Arizona, and that gave me the opportunity to select the books that would go on its shelves.

I made a less-than-wise choice as a young mother when I became deeply engrossed in playing bridge. I played several afternoons a week and enjoyed it immensely. Then Elder Melvin J. Ballard came to stake conference and called upon us to put aside our bridge games. At first I rebelled and then acquiesced, finally realizing how much time that I could better use otherwise I had been giving up to the game. It was a test of obedience. I chose to obey.

I make no pretensions at perfection. People sometimes assume that because I am the President's wife I must already have arrived at that state, but I struggle every day with the same kinds of imperfections you all do. There is no place so high that it is beyond difficulty or temptation. They are part of the human condition.

It is a truism that the Lord does not judge us by what we have but by what we do with what we have. The rich may be haughty, the poor envious, the powerful cruel, the weak sniveling. And those between the extremes may well be complacent and lukewarm.

The scriptures remind us that for men "to be learned is good if they hearken unto the counsels of God" (2 Ne. 9:29).

To be rich is good, if you can be humble. To be learned is good if you can be wise. To be healthy is good if you can be useful. To be beautiful is good if you can be gracious.

There is, however, nothing inherently bad in being poor, unlettered, sickly, or plain.

To be poor is good, if you can still be generous of spirit. To be unschooled is good, if it motivates you to be curious. To be sickly is good, if it helps you have compassion. To be plain is good, if it saves you from vanity.

Every life is full of challenges. I know something of losing one's parents, of seeing one's spouse racked with stress and pain, of having one's savings of many years wiped out by theft or bank failure, of watching loved ones stray from the gospel, of having a child stricken with crippling illness, and of feeling disabling old age creeping on.

Your challenges may be different but no easier. They may involve the high cost of honesty, the impulse of inappropriate sexual involvement, worldly activities that try to crowd out time for prayer and gospel study, disappointment in people you thought you could trust, the collapse of dearly held dreams.

Remember that no trial is too great, no task too hard, for you and the Lord together. I pray for us all that we may measure up to the challenges that come to us. I pray that we will have knowledge and wisdom to make right choices. I pray that we will accept the great atoning sacrifice of Jesus Christ, so that he may draw us up and share with us his great eternal work. And I ask these things in his holy name. Amen.

Decisions Determine Our Destiny

Hugh W. Pinnock

> Elder Hugh W. Pinnock is now serving as general president of the Sunday School and has been a member of the First Quorum of Seventy since October of 1977. His previous Church positions have included that of bishop, high councilor, member of the Priesthood Leadership Committee, mission president, and member of several other committees.
>
> Elder Pinnock was educated at the University of Utah, where he served as president of each class before being elected student body president.
>
> As a businessman in the Intermountain Area, he has served on several boards of directors, as president of a number of life insurance and marketing organizations, as a founder of several businesses, and as general agent for the Connecticut Mutual Life Insurance Company. He is a Chartered Life Underwriter and a life member of the Million Dollar Round Table. He is also a life member of the Life Managers Association.
>
> Elder Pinnock has served as a chairman of the American Cancer Association, the University of Utah Alumni Association, and recently as president of the LDS Hospital-Deseret Foundation.
>
> He is married to Anne Hawkins, and they are the parents of six children.

As I look out over this great group of women, I think of the words penned in Joel 3:14: "Multitudes, multitudes in the valley of decision." And it was John Milton who accurately stated about women, "Oh fairest of creation! Last and best of all God's works!" (*Paradise Lost,* 9.896-97.)

As I stand here today, a number of thoughts cross my mind. How much more comfortable I would be if we could sit, just three or four of us, in my office and talk about decision making in your lives and in the Kingdom and about the way our decisions determine our destinies. If my words seem a little more personal than would normally be spoken before a congregation this size, please bear with me and realize that I am trying to imagine you in a much more individual setting than where we are in now. I simply can be more effective if I consider us as speaking one to one, spirit to spirit, than in any other format.

The title suggested for my talk this morning is "Decisions Determine Our Destiny." This topic is not unlike a statement Agnes DeMille wrote: "No trumpets sound when the important decisions of our lives are made. Destiny is made known silently." (*Dance to the Piper* [Boston: Little,

Brown, 1952].) One of America's great military leaders said, "A decision is the action a person must take when he has information so incomplete that the answer does not suggest itself" (Arthur William Radford, chairman of the Joint Chiefs of Staff, in *Time*, 25 February 1957).

There are some generalities about decision making that need to be stated. What is the universal business of our Heavenly Father's children? It is being decision makers. Uncertainty and Satan's lifestyle have been and will continue to be our opponents. Overcoming uncertainty and sin is our mission. Whether the outcome is joy-filled and eternally satisfying depends on the end result of the moment of decision. Yes, the moment of decision is, without a doubt, the most creative and critical event in our lives. May our decisions open windows onto a wider world, one that conforms more to our Heavenly Father's will.

There are a number of decisions in life that, because of their opaqueness, we may not make, or at least not early enough. For instance, the happiest relationships with which I am familiar are those in which a wife and husband allow each other great freedom, a secretary and her employer operate largely independently of one another, a department chairman allows all who labor in that department maximum flexibility, or a parent, through trust, allows a child a great deal of freedom. Isn't this one of those decisions that we must make—to associate whenever possible with those who allow us to fly free? This is the plan of our Heavenly Father, you know. Ideally, each member of a couple in love frees the other to climb, to grow, and to improve righteously—without restrictions. Rita Boumy Pappas observed this when she wrote, "I did not let them nail my soul as they do butterflies." (*Roxanne*, 1975).

The scriptures teach, and I have learned, that we get from life pretty much what we want. But, every so often, we must see what we get before we know what we have wanted. Alma taught, "For I know that [the Lord] granteth unto men according to their desire, whether it be unto death or unto life; yea, I know that he allotteth unto men according to their wills" (Alma 29:4).

A young woman I know slipped into my office one day. She was agitated and upset. Naturally, I asked, "What is wrong?"

"I hate my job, the night class I am taking is boring, and I haven't had a date since the Saints left Nauvoo!" she exclaimed.

"What is wrong at work? You applied for that job, and when you got it you were delighted."

"Well, it isn't too bad," she admitted. "In fact," her voice trailed off, "it really isn't bad at all. It really is just what I want. I guess I've just become a bit discouraged."

"What about the night class you elected to take after studying the catalog for two weeks?" I asked.

She reached the same conclusion.

"Isn't the dating game where most of your real frustrations lie?"

"Yes," she admitted.

"What are you doing about it?" I asked.

"Nothing," she admitted.

We then discussed her responsibility to assume some control in this area of her life, for there is much she can legitimately do to correct this condition. Wouldn't we be wiser if, under the coolness of in-tune thoughts, we decided what we wanted and then worked for it?

Many decisions each of us makes involve others intimately and perhaps eternally. While dealing with a group of priesthood leaders I discovered that if a decision carried some trappings of control or strategy or inflexibility, those called upon to put the decision into action would not respond enthusiastically, even though they felt out of duty that they should. How best, I wondered to myself, can these decisions be communicated so as to improve their chance of being adopted? Partly out of frustration and partly out of deep respect for these men, I suggested that the ideas I wanted to share with them should *not* be added to their own procedures or supersede their own ideas unless they seemed to be more effective than what was being used. I asked them to use these ideas very, very selectively, and only if they would help these men in their own ministry. I attempted to introduce a level of spontaneity, allowing them complete freedom.

I was pleased to observe, approximately six weeks later, that each of the decisions had been carried through to an accomplished objective. Moreover, others with whom these leaders had communicated seemed almost as enthusiastic as the leaders over the new technique. When our decisions involve others, not only do we need to be highly flexible in encouraging their implementation, but we should provide a supportive and empathetic environment in which they can be used.

Maria Millis loved Jesus. She was a kitchen maid in the home of nobility and befriended a little boy in the mansion where she labored. His name was Anthony Ashley Cooper, but history knows him as the Earl of Shaftsbury. He inherited the title from his father, who gave him everything—except love. His mother, a social butterfly, ignored the needs of her little boy.

Each night Maria would bring him a plate of cookies and a glass of milk. While he enjoyed these simple refreshments she would tell him of God's great love and of the sacrifice of Jesus, and she would encourage him to kneel and pray before going to bed. Maria became a second mother to young Anthony. He would confide in her concerning his problems, and she would then counsel and soothe him—something his own parents would not do.

Young Anthony might have grown up to be like his father—a nasty man, a heavy drinker, with little interest in family affairs. But instead, thanks to Maria's tutoring and love, he became a godly young man, sickened at the wretched social conditions of England's poor in the early nineteenth century. She acquainted him with oppression, with poverty, and with slum conditions; and she informed him that many children were forced to work fourteen hours a day in mines and mills with no opportunity for schooling.

Young Lord Ashley never departed from Maria's influence. He became a member of Parliament, and for years he championed the cause of working people. Because he was wealthy he was able to give all his time to promoting reform. Determined to remove the blight of England's slums, he championed housing projects, and, despite the bitter antagonism of the profiteers, he abolished the employment of women and children in mines and sponsored an act that prohibited small boys from working as chimney sweeps.

What gave Lord Ashley the courage to persist in his reform efforts? He said it was the memory of Maria Millis's devotion to him as a boy. From this servant lady he had learned justice based on the love of Jesus. When opposition was particularly injurious and fierce and he became discouraged, he would reach inside his waistcoat and feel the watch Maria had given him years before. Her faith brought courage and strength to his heart.

During his lifelong crusades for social improvement, Lord Ashley endured many social snubs. He was often shunned because of his concerns for those unable to defend their own rights. But when he died ninety-four years ago, even his archenemies walked to Westminster Abbey in tribute to his faith and devotion. Two hundred religious, social, and philanthropic organizations were officially represented at his memorial service. How different everything might have been if a Christian kitchen maid had not befriended a frightened little boy by bringing him cookies and teaching him about Jesus.

Sometimes we have to accept ourselves as we are before our decisions can lead us to greater success. A lovely lady was living a good life. She had a sound marriage, a job she loved, some mature children, a host of friends, and several fascinating hobbies. Her health was good and her future was secure. She was not unhappy, but she was not content. As she approached her middle years, she took pride in her family and in what she had accomplished in several Church callings, but she wanted to do so much more. Mostly, she wanted to write. She had started many articles, writing and rewriting the initial paragraph and had even begun working on a book or two. She became ridden with guilt over the fact that she was not accomplishing what she had hoped her decisions would lead her to.

She taught a group of graduate students who were counseling interns. Many would tape their counseling sessions. One day a student shared his tape with the class. As they listened, they heard the heartbreak of a young woman tortured by feelings of inadequacy. She spoke of dissatisfaction with her physical appearance, of her shyness, and of doubting her scholastic capacity. The student stopped the tape and observed, "This young woman was a top student in her high school class. She had many friends and served as student body vice-president. She was popular and was generally regarded as the top young lady of her age in the little town where she lived. She was highly respected as a college student. And yet, she seems to feel inferior to her peers." A member of the class broke in: "That gal just hasn't learned yet that you don't have to be perfect to be darn good."

That you don't have to be perfect to be darn good is an obvious fact, but it deeply affected the professor. She, in a series of reveries, thought of other students, professors, brothers and sisters in her ward, and others who, because of their own decisions, were nowhere near what they should have been. Other memories crowded in: attractive women who responded to compliments by denying them, musicians who resisted playing their instruments or singing for fear of being criticized. She realized that many people's responses communicated that if you are not perfect, you are no good at all. She thought of her self-doubts and the despair she felt over her own expectations. Even when others were applauding her achievements, she recalled the guilt and frustration she had endured through the years because she wanted to be perfect too early in this great eternal experience.

She resolved to write whenever she could, and as well as she knew how. She accepted the fact that she would never produce the perfect novel, the finest poem, or an ever-enduring document. But a few years later she did view with satisfaction a number of published works and smiled a bit nostalgically at the vital lesson she had learned from one of her many students.

Just as managers are hired because they have displayed the potential for making astute decisions, all of us have found and will continue to find ourselves standing upon the ground our feet have taken us to by following certain decisions. Leaders everywhere are judged on their "decision wins," and we, in eternity, will be judged on the number of winning decisions we make.

There is some double-barreled wisdom in Frederick Amiel's statement that "the man who insists upon seeing with perfect clearness before he decides, never decides." He then said, "Accept life, and you must accept regret. All of our decisions will not be perfect. We will feel, hopefully temporarily, regret. But let us never wait for perfect clarity." (*Book of Unusual Quotations,* ed. Rudolf Flesch [New York: Harper, 1957], p. 56.)

It would be a rare decision indeed for which all of the data is apparent in perfect clarity before the decision is made. Some of our greatest growth comes from the mind-stretching exercise of filling in where information is not available and weighing that which is incomplete. Sometimes, there must simply be a leap of faith. As we read the Doctrine and Covenants, it becomes obvious that the Lord wanted Joseph Smith and the Church to build precept upon precept, concept upon concept, for that is how decisions are structured. Indeed, Moroni stated, "Wherefore, dispute not because ye see not, for ye receive no witness until after the trial of your faith" (Ether 12:6).

Decision making is the specific task of life. No one can avoid it. Within the Church, we are to start with what is right, rather than what is acceptable or comfortable. I see many people searching for life's answers outside the gospel of Christ. Yet, almost every thoughtful person knows that anyone who follows the Master's teachings will invariably be happy.

Looking for a decision-making system outside of the gospel is a little like doing what a man named Nasrudin did in a story found in the folklore of the Middle East. He was searching for something in the dirt near the front door of his home when an acquaintance came by and inquired, "Nasrudin, what have you lost?"

"My house key," said Nasrudin.

In an attempt to help, the friend went down upon his knees and they both looked intently for it. After a few minutes the acquaintance asked, "Just exactly where did you drop it?"

"In my house," answered Nasrudin.

"Then why are you looking here, Nasrudin?"

"There is more light here than inside my house."

This little story is old and worn, yet it has a timeless message. If the gospel holds the answers for us, why look elsewhere? That simple concept is the foundation of all that I will say this day. "The earth is the Lord's, and the fulness thereof; the world, and they that dwell therein" (Psalms 24:1).

We know this is true because one of the more effective keys in the making of decisions is to simply ask, "What would happen if everyone made the same decision that I am making." We can ask that question whether it relates to additional schooling, ironing out troubled relationships, or serving more effectively in a Church position. By thinking of the world, the Church, the ward, our neighborhood, or our family, we are more easily able to determine what is best for us personally. In other words, can you or I make a decision that would not lead to a more effective and peaceful family, ward, university, or Church? No, because the gospel is universal, and therefore gospel-oriented decisions will have universal applicability. This concept is not unlike the Golden Rule. Whenever our decisions are good for others they are right for us.

I was reading recently that computer specialists have found a number of problems that man, no matter how unskilled he might be, can solve more effectively than can a computer. An example of this is working out an itinerary for visiting ten cities. Even though we can feed all of the data into a computer, which sometimes requires great time and expense, we find that by simply looking at a map, our own observations can solve that problem better and more quickly. Despite the broad applications of computers, the decisions we make that are most vital to our happiness do not lend themselves to computer or checklist solutions. Nothing can replace one's "feel for something."

Each of us carries a visceral antenna that is at least as valid in determining what needs to be done or what decision needs to be made as the scientific method. No, let me correct that. This visceral antenna is more substantial and exact than formulas, checklists, or predefined procedures in so much of what really matters. This "feel" is eternal in nature. It is God-given. It is light. But also remember, sisters, that it operates only in the environment of righteous exercise of free agency. "Ye are free," Samuel the Lamanite taught the Nephites, "And now remember, remember, my brethren, that whosoever perisheth, perisheth unto himself; and whosoever doeth iniquity, doeth it unto himself; for behold ye are free; ye are permitted to act for yourselves; for behold, God hath given unto you a knowledge and he hath made you free" (Hel. 14:30).

What decisions of life do we need to make in order to return to a smiling Father in Heaven?

First, be yourself. One of the most strategic of all decisions is the decision to be yourself, while always striving to be a better self. Perhaps the whole concept of free agency is built upon this principle. Don't even think about being somebody else! You are unique; you are good; you have unlimited potential. Just decide to be better.

Second, as men and women, sisters and brothers, we are to walk together. There is no other way because it is God's way. Thank goodness for gender differences. The most sacred act of eternity is accomplished through that partnership with our Heavenly Father as spirits are given bodies. When inequalities because of sex are observed we are to do what we can to correct them, together.

A lovely young lady came to me upset with her bishop because of some perceived disparaging remark he had made relating to sisters in general and her in particular. "What can I do to remedy this uncomfortable situation?" she asked. "Go to him," I replied. "He has unrighteously offended you." In such situations we should always follow the Savior's advice:

> Moreover if thy brother shall trespass against thee, go and tell him his fault between thee and him alone: if he shall hear thee, thou hast gained thy brother.
>
> But if he will not hear thee, then take with thee one or two more, that in the mouth of two or three witnesses every word may be established.
>
> And if he shall neglect to hear them, tell it unto the church: but if he neglect to hear the church, let him be unto thee as an heathen man and a publican. [Matt. 18:15-17]
>
> Ye have heard that it hath been said, An eye for an eye, and a tooth for a tooth:
>
> But I say unto you, That ye resist not evil: but whosoever shall smite thee on thy right cheek, turn to him the other also.
>
> And if any man will sue thee at the law, and take away thy coat, let him have thy cloak also.
>
> And whosoever shall compel thee to go a mile, go with him twain.
>
> Give to him that asketh thee, and from him that would borrow of thee turn not thou away.
>
> Ye have heard that it hath been said, Thou shalt love thy neighbour, and hate thine enemy.
>
> But I say unto you, Love your enemies, bless them that curse you, ... and pray for them which despitefully use you, and persecute you;
>
> That ye may be the children of your Father which is in heaven: for he maketh his sun to rise on the evil and on the good, and sendeth rain on the just and on the unjust.
>
> For if ye love them which love you, what reward have ye? do not

> even the publicans the same?
> And if ye salute your brethren only, what do ye more than others? do not even the publicans so?
> Be ye therefore perfect, even as your Father which is in heaven is perfect. [Matt. 5:38-48]

Nobel Prize winner Albert Camus said, "Don't walk in front of me; I may not follow. Don't walk behind me; I may not lead. Just walk beside me and be my friend." May we decide in our interactions not to make gender the deciding factor in determining how we will handle a relationship.

Third, learn from the past, but concentrate upon today. Have we realized more than superficially that we cannot, except by repentance, alter the past? Each of us, however, can dramatically change what will happen to us this afternoon and in the future. For example, could any decision be as important as living the commandments? Many years ago in a tiny village nestled among the Rockies there lived a grand old man who was well into his eighties. He had come through the storms and stresses of a lifetime, but his spirit was strong and his mind alert. Each Sunday he went to the chapel and taught a class of single adults. One Sunday, in a reflective mood, he interjected into his lesson: "An important thing I have learned from life thus far is the truth of an old proverb: 'Never forget in the dark what God has told you in the light.'" Let us decide in the "light" what we must remember not to forget when temptations, stressful times, or problems come. "All things work together for good for those who love God."

I hope we are over the silly belief that when a problem is defined and a solution determined one does not have much work to do. For that is when all real effort begins. A number of years ago, a wonderful musician residing in Salt Lake City decided she would not do anything that would remove her from an eventual home with her Father in Heaven and from a meaningful relationship with her eldest brother, the Savior. Another goal she had was to be married, although she relegated this beneath the other two. The years came and went quickly, as they do. A number of years after her initial decisions, her fortieth birthday came and went. Four additional years quickly passed. Everywhere she went people were made happier, lives were blessed, music was enjoyed. She became closer to her Father in Heaven than she had ever been before. The Master became her best friend. Just last Saturday a convert from Delaware, while in the temple, asked her to marry him. All that she had worked for was now hers as she replied, yes. So many times when the night was late, she had been tempted to leave her decisions behind at least temporarily and to walk on foreign soil. She did not. Time often does play an important part in decisions.

Fourth, decide to communicate openly. Recently I read that a religious organization and a group of unwed mothers have had a number of buttons made which simply read, "No." In a cartoon advertisement relating to their distribution, two girls are talking about how they can reject the sexual advances of their dates. One girl tells the other, "Wear a 'No' button and then the men will only ask out those who will participate." The next frame shows a young man asking where he can obtain his "No" button. Far too often our communications about our decisions are not as clear as they need to be. Think how helpful it might be if each of us could wear proudly upon a collar, blouse, jacket, or shirt a label reflecting the decisions we have made that would regulate other people's interactions with us. But, dear sisters, that is not possible. Perhaps the lesson to be learned from the "No" button campaign is that we must all be more *open* and *exact* as we communicate our decisions and intentions to others.

Fifth, be careful about making decisions as "a matter of principle." A lovely lady served in an important position for a number of years. She had made some errors, but they did not justify terminating her employment. At her retirement time, however, the man who ran the business decided not to reward her with the customary farewell party. When asked by others why he was not giving her a party and a gift, he said, "You must realize, it's a matter of principle. She made some mistakes that cost me money."

How sad, I thought. More important "principles" would dictate that she had done well and that she deserved a party and a gift. But he could only see the one or two costly yet innocent mistakes she had made. I questioned his principles, knowing that a number of his people were not being paid a fair rate of income. His decisions had been based on a "matter of principle," but it was his "principle" and certainly not the Lord's.

In a distant city, a man serving as a bishop will not invite a frightened daughter home for Thanksgiving or Christmas because she has done things of which he has not approved. A "matter of principle," he says. But isn't the principle of loving and forgiving seventy times seven a higher one?

Another bitter, elderly sister has not attended church for seven years. When asked why, she exclaims, "It is a matter of principle." An auxiliary leader had been impatient with her and had hurt her feelings. A "matter of principle"? No. The ice is too thin when our only justification for behavior is simply a "matter of principle."

Sixth, go on from where you are now and courageously make the best of things. As I was counseling a young lady recently, I asked her why she had done something that was rather foolish. "Because I had made the decision," she answered, "and didn't think I should change it." We should not cling to wrong decisions. We understand the law of repentance. If we need to change directions, then let's do it.

Seventh, avoid making a "big deal" of every little challenge that comes along. I remember some missionaries in the mission field for whom transfering to a new city was earthshaking. Some elders and sisters would become almost overwhelmed with each month as it raced by, particularly in the last year, where every day became a time warp and every communication "life shattering." It recently occurred to me, though, that the happy and significantly helpful people walk through life without making "big deals" of their decisions and circumstances. In fact, they often do all within their power to avoid a "big deal."

Dear sisters, isn't this how life should be lived? I watch the Brethren transferred around the world, causing dramatic changes in their lives and the lives of their families, and yet they treat it as no big deal. I have seen mission presidents accomplish incredible results, sometimes improving baptisms by four or five times while seeing even more mature and helpful investigators come into the Church. And yet nothing is said, nor do they want anything said. They simply do what is right, and it is no "big deal." Perhaps an important decision that many of us need to make is to live the type of life in which no "big deal" is expected or desired.

Eighth, decide to be part of what is going on. This is a decision that might pay higher dividends than many others we could make; it is the epitome of maintaining perspective.

Dr. Ernest A. Fitzgerald, a minister in Winston-Salem, North Carolina, reported that many years ago a visitor to western North Carolina decided that a certain part of that mountain country was ideally suited for growing grapes. Determined to open a business, he tried to get the people of that community involved in his venture. He met with resistance and a singular lack of interest. Finally, in desperation, he called these mountain people together and made a slick sales pitch. "Join me," he pleaded with the natives. "In three or four years you will be so well fixed you will never have to worry again." There was a long and heavy silence among these folk; then one oldtimer drawled, "I ain't worrying none now."

All of us know people like that. They remain tranquil and poised despite the pressures of the moment. Other people may become excited and stampede into unwise decisions, but these folks take the longer look and make their judgments wisely.

A great-aunt became a favorite of mine as she tended us during the growing-up years. At the time she did not impress me as being profound, yet many of my own feelings and directions have come from her attitude, which, until very recently, I could not define. She was simply part of what was going on. She was as much of the environment as the air we breathed or the water we drank. We almost didn't know she was there, yet none of us ever will forget her. Perhaps a vital decision each of us could make is to be in harmony with what surrounds us.

Living in our neighborhood is a delightful woman who spends a great percentage of her time helping those who have found themselves in unfortunate circumstances. My wife returned home the other day to report that this dear sister had broken her leg and had required some extensive orthopedic work. My wife, remembering the many kind deeds this lovely woman had performed for others, took dinner to the family. Sister Donnel Hansen looked up and said, "You know, there's a time to help, and a time to receive help. I accept whatever my Heavenly Father decides for me. Thank you for bringing food into our home at this time." What a lovely and mature way to live.

While I was visiting in the office of a member of the Twelve quite recently, we talked about the type of person who could fill a certain position of vital responsibility. I said, "What we need for that position is a real 'tiger.'"

"No tiger or fireball for me!" he exclaimed. "Fireballs burn out too quickly. Let's find a person who knows how to handle the ups and downs. We should be able to work with this person for many years, if necessary. The fireballs give off a lot of heat and light, but they usually burn out quickly. The people who are geared for the long pull keep this unpredictable world from tearing apart." Yes, we want those who are a part of what is going on, who comfortably fit in.

Ninth, avoid being forced into hurried decisions. Many people have become alarmed to learn that there is a "constituency for inflation." Yes, certain people not only benefit from inflation and the dollar's loss in value, but do anything they can to perpetuate this plague in America. Even more obvious is the fact that a number of people benefit from decisions that are hurried or are less than rational. Sometimes certain decisions that are made as directional guides for the *future* are, in fact, silly justifications for the *past*.

Haven't we all noticed that too much haste or too much of anything is simply too much? Blaise Pascal said, "Our senses can grasp nothing that is in extreme." Too much noise deafens us; too much light blinds us; too great a distance and too much proximity equally prevent us from being able to see.

Speed in making up one's mind could become a technique for avoiding decision making. Dr. Joyce Brothers stated that though the quick decision creates an illusion of command, a lightning choice may mean only that someone has snatched at the handy alternative rather than coming to grips with the real issue. In other words, are some of our "slick and quick" decisions simply our avoidance of the facts? Perhaps this very day is a time to rethink our quick decisions.

Tenth, identify and use appropriate support systems. If I were attending a men's week at Brigham Young University, speaking before a body of men the size of this beautiful group of women, my words and thoughts, at least for part of my presentation, would touch upon organizational items and responsibilities such as bearing the priesthood honorably and quorum responsibilities. As I feel your spirit, I am impressed to talk of the importance of the weekly experience of Relief Society.

I cannot share what means the most in decision making without sharing with you the importance of obtaining the pespectives, joy, and blessings that come from the structure provided by the Relief Society. It is God's organization for women. Just as structure is important in a building, as the engineering design accommodates stresses and strains that time and weather bring, so each of you good sisters must weave into your life this structure that will provide part of your support system, making you what you are and able to cope with the events that will come.

Each of us also has the responsibility to be part of the support system, especially spiritually, but temporally where needed. The decisions we make lead to our support systems. Other support systems that provide structure in our lives are our families, callings, avocations, friends, and other things that motivate us. May we choose wisely? What places afford the most comfort in time of need? It is there we will return to touch, to refill, and to rethink. Where are your havens? They are your support systems. Define them carefully.

Now, I would like to discuss, in closing, the components of eternal decisions. When discouragement or depression slips into our lives or when we feel that we are enveloped in sickness, our ailment usually is not as much an illness as a case of finding ourselves unwell. A body that is out of condition and out of tune can be definably not sick, but at the same time we certainly cannot consider it to be well. Likewise, many of our decisions are not sick or evil, but they might be decisions that are not well. How can we decide more accurately what needs to be done, thought, and experienced?

First, our decisions must be viable eternally. If a decision cannot be seen in an eternal perspective, we should decide not to make it. We must determine whether our short-range achievements are consistent with our Heavenly Father's long-range objectives for us. Effective decisions of today must dovetail with the "big picture" of forever. Eternal decision making needs to facilitate the flow of joy. One must sacrifice his future for the momentary gains or pleasures of the present. Look far down the road to determine where the proposed course will lead. The people who take the long view manage to live life at its best.

Second, share with Deity, through prayer, the matters that need decisions. Patience becomes critical with most answers to prayer. Our Heavenly Father obviously wears a wrist watch that ticks at a different rate than ours does. Often his answers come in the form of, "Not now, my child. Later."

Only too often people feel that the Supreme Being is removed from their lives, through sin or for other reasons. This reminds me of an 1851 newspaper headline that reportedly appeared in the British press soon after the first channel cable linking England with mainland Europe had broken. The headline read, "The Continent Is Isolated" (Franz Ulrich, in *Forbes,* 19 Jan. 1981, p. 23). We cannot remove God from our lives, but we can remove ourselves from his holy influence. We are to let him know we need his help. He is there. Talk to him. "He will guide you into all truth" (See John 16:13).

Third, listen and be logical. If your petition is unique, then don't be surprised if you, under inspiration, receive a unique answer; but also don't be surprised if you get an answer that is obvious and timeworn.

Revelation is a gift that is yours and mine. Inspiration is a gift of the Spirit and is to be valued and sought after. Remember, however, that much of what happens in life relating to decisions does not come from special inspiration. It comes from simply being a member of the kingdom of God, blessed with sound doctrine to guide us. We do not need a revelation on whether to remain virtuous, or whether to pay our tithing. Those decisions have been made before. We do need to decide to remain strong, however, and to follow our prophet.

In making a decision, we must avoid "any odor of hypocrisy." There cannot even be a subtle smell of something that is not right.

Because "no" is often the best answer, let us accept it as such. As a young businessman I was offered a wonderful opportunity, or so I thought. It was exciting! Everything pointed to it as being the perfect business situation. After I prayed for several days, however, the Spirit said, "No." With hesitancy and disappointment, I said, "No." I remember how bad I felt, turning down a position that any businessman would have given almost all for. Within a year, though, I learned that the opportunity had soured. My whole life would have been dramatically different had I said yes.

Fourth, seek input from the words of our prophet, from the scriptures, from lovely and respected sisters and brothers in the kingdom—from any source that is God-inspired and part of this great kingdom. As President Marion G. Romney said, "It is my opinion that the Latter-day Saints, because of the knowledge they have received in the revelations, are better prepared to meet the perplexities of our times than any other people" (in Conference Report, 30 Sept. 1961).

Fifth, exert enough energy to make the decision work. The fact that "work" or "works" are mentioned not less than 785 times in ancient and modern scriptures is not an accident. The Savior said, "If any man will *do* God's will, he shall know" (John 7:17; italics added).

Out of our decisions are born deeds. Out of our deeds we form habits. Out of these habits grows our character. And it is on our character, of course, that we build our destiny.

To all these things I humbly testify.

Choices in a Nation of Alternatives

Paula Hawkins

Senator Paula Hawkins (R-Florida) is one of two women currently serving in the United States Senate and is the first Latter-day Saint woman to do so. Her political career spans over twenty years and includes involvement with organizations such as the PTA, the Heart Fund, and the Cancer Society as well as a twelve-year membership on the Republican National Committee. She served on the Florida State Public Service Commission from 1973 to 1979 and as chair of that body from 1977 to 1979. Her efforts as a member of that Commission on behalf of the consumer obviously won the confidence of Floridians as she was elected to the Senate last year by a comfortable margin from a field of twelve candidates.

A native of Salt Lake City, Senator Hawkins was raised in Georgia and attended Utah State University. She is married to Walter Eugene Hawkins, who graduated from Georgia Tech as an electronics engineer and is currently a partner in an electronics firm in the Orlando, Florida, area. As the spouse of Senator Paul Hawkins, Brother Hawkins is in the unique position of being the first "Senate Husband." An active member of the Church, Brother Hawkins has served in a range of ward and stake positions. The Hawkins are the parents of three children.

This morning at breakfast I told the people assembled there that I was born in Salt Lake City, but that I lived there only until I could take control of my family, which was about seven months later. Then we left Utah and moved all over the United States. My father was in the Navy, and in those days the Navy moved a lot and the family went along. We didn't know that a family could stay in one place to avoid hurting the children by changing communities on them so much. I was really raised in Atlanta, Georgia, and I consider myself a Southern girl, but I did go to Utah State University and am very proud of my Utah roots, my Utah heritage, and the pioneer spirit that I think I still bear.

I am excited about our topic, "Ye Are Free to Choose." We are free to choose and subscribe to those beliefs that we want to in this country; we can be very loud about it or we can be very quiet about it, but we can pursue our beliefs in a country that gives us the freedoms and the opportunities that this country does. This is the only country in the world that I know of where people are still so free. I think we must treat tenderly and carefully the freedoms we take for granted. As we read the daily newspapers, we could make a long list of countries whose citizens have lost the opportunity to choose anything—their form of government, where they live, how much they make, what education they get, what pursuits they will follow.

It has become common in my state of Florida for human beings to drift ashore after living in boats in horrible conditions for fifty to one hundred fifty days, trying to reach the United States—and freedom. The first thing they say, in broken English, is "Is this America?" Despite all the trappings of the civilized world that we have, the electronic communications equipment that can instantly bring war right into our living rooms every night at six and allow us to be armchair generals, the most desirable thing in the eyes and minds of those who are drifting to our shores is freedom. We have accepted over one hundred forty thousand of these people in my state in the last few months, and it has become a tremendous problem to share these burdens equitably. I tell the other senators that we want to be able to receive all these people, but we must also give them opportunities and responsibilities.

People are not born United States senators; we are all born alike. There is great equality in the nursery. Character is then formed block by block, precept by precept. Your lifetime is a mosaic of small quilt blocks, like the ones my grandmother made of small pieces of different fabrics that, in the end, will make a great coverlet you can wrap yourself in and be identified with. Every stitch and every piece of fabric is part of the character you are going to have.

The advent of the electronic media has exchanged character for charisma in political campaigns and has greatly changed the electoral process. But I believe that this year, for the first time, people saw through the celluloid, cookie-cutter people who were running for office throughout the United States and chose for themselves the leadership qualities and the kind of leaders they had been yearning for as this ship of state drifted without strong, firm leadership.

There never has been a time that I remember when we have had so many problems. As I make a list of things I should do as a senator from Florida, I find an endless number of problems that need solving. But we need new solutions just as we have needed new leadership.

I became active in political life in 1956. Because I was from the "solid South," I had never seen a real live Republican until I moved to Florida. I had been raised in a state where everyone was a Democrat, and I did not understand what the two-party system was supposed to be. When my husband and I moved to Florida, we found that everyone had to register by party. When we went down to register and the registrar asked, "Which party are you going to register in?" I thought she was the nosiest woman I had ever met in my life. I said it was none of her business. She said she didn't mean to intrude, but that there was a blank on the registration form for "party" and in Florida you had to choose. Suddenly I found myself free to choose the primary in which I wanted to participate.

I said to the registrar, "I am a Republican." My husband said, "You are? When did all this happen?" And the lady said, "Now if you do that, I must tell you you'll never be able to vote in Florida."

I thought, "I'll show her," and I wrote down "Republican" because I was free to choose a different kind of leadership. I wanted to choose between people and between parties, and I thought that if there were no strong two-party system in the state of Florida, I'd start one.

That lady was right. I didn't vote for about eight years in Florida except in national elections. A Republican never ran for school board, for sheriff, or for anything; and I couldn't vote because the machine had been locked. It made me so angry not to be allowed to choose the party whose platform I agreed with the most (and we all can differ; in fact, you should never sign up until you know what you are signing up for) that I decided we were going to offer a choice to the people of Florida.

From that humble beginning—when we were literally locked out of the ballot box and stood around the little city hall of Maitland, grumbling because a few of us couldn't participate in the voting—we built a strong two-party system. Of course, there's been a lot of fighting involved, which is only natural. (My husband says I can start a fight in an empty room. Those are the ones I win, by the way.)

When we had two small children and were building our first house, I decided my little community really needed sewers. We learned that everyone had septic tanks in this small community, and with the vision of youth we asked, "Why don't we have a sewer system?"

The mayor said, "No way can you have a sewer system. We all have septic tanks in this community"—even though we all lived on a lake—"and you can have a septic tank just like we do."

I decided that if the mayor wouldn't change his mind, we would change the mayor. So we organized a small group called the "dirty dozen." We all pushed strollers with small children in them, and our great aim was to get a sewer system in my city because it was something we needed every day; the water system was vital to all of our lives and our life-styles.

We found out that the mayor and two councilmen were running for reelection about two months from the very day our request for a sewer system was turned down, so we found our own candidates for those three positions, we seated all three, and we got the sewer system. One reason for this is that we got a commitment from each candidate before we ran him that he would favor installing sewers. One mistake many people make is that they don't get a commitment from candidates before supporting them; they work hard and then are very disappointed when the elected official doesn't do what they expected, because they didn't get that commitment. But we got it at the outset, got that sewer system installed, and had the lowest water and sewer bills in the state of Florida until just this last year. We put our system in back when capital costs were low and the streets weren't paved. We didn't have to dig up cement to put the pipes in, and acting early proved to be a great saving for those people who eventually moved to my small town of three hundred and swelled its population to about ten thousand. We were able to put in that sewer system because of vision and fortitude, because of a great desire to fight for what is right, and because we could choose whether we wanted sewer systems or not.

It was 1958 when we finally won that battle. My husband says it serves me right that in 1972 I was elected to the Public Service Commission, a statewide elected office in Florida which regulated, among other things, 900 water and sewer companies. That's the awfullest work in the world. But that is part of the American dream. One day you can be a housewife, petitioning your city council or your county commission to do something you think is in the best interest of the community, and the next day you may be the candidate for an office that will in fact offer choices to others.

I don't think there is anything complicated about government; I don't think it's mysterious. I think some people like to make it seem that way. There are no duties a mayor of a community is involved in that aren't the concerns of the mother of the household or the family in that house. Families are concerned with education, with where to empty the garbage, with where their children are going to play, and with the traffic patterns during school and work rush hours. Expand all those family interests to a larger circle, and you find that the mayor is really the mama of the town.

I did a study for the Commission on the Status of Women in 1966 and found that the smaller the community, the more apt it was to have all women officials. But as a town got larger, it started electing men because people thought that when responsibilities became greater public offices should go to men. I think, though, that this depends on the qualities of the individual. There are no elected offices that specify male or female; they are merited strictly on the basis of ability and capacity to work and communicate.

Early in 1972 we discussed whether I would run for statewide office in Florida. There are a lot of people there, it's very expensive to campaign, and I was a member of the minority party. Even though I had gotten the two-party system going, we were still a minority party and are to this day, outnumbered two to one by the Democratic ranks, although some have had the vision to choose Republicans to represent them even though they stay registered in the other party. My husband has said he has but one wife to give to his country, and he told many people after we won that first election that the only reason he decided I could run was because he thought I would lose.

That was in 1972. We received 1.2 million votes after spending only $60,000—a historical landmark for our state because it was the lowest ratio of campaign cost to number of votes ever for that office. And the position was an awful job. That commission regulated monopolies—electric companies, telephone companies, water and sewer companies, and all transportation in my state.

In 1976 I ran for reelection, and, as in 1972, the press dubbed me the "housewife from Maitland." It was intended as a put-down, but I decided it was a great title—I don't know of a harder job to do well than that of being a housewife—so I grabbed that title and ran on it. We won reelection in 1976 with 1.4 million votes. We had added to our 1972 margin even though we had a record to defend then, a defense made very difficult by the Arab oil embargo. A lot of people thought I started that fight, too, but I had nothing to do with the increase in the price of oil. What I did have a lot to do with was the giving of refunds to every rate payer in the state of Florida because there had been some illegal passing of funds between the utility company officials and the oil procurers. The producers of "60 Minutes" became very interested in the fact that someone in an elected position would be honest enough to expose the corruption she saw, even though it meant fighting her own commission and her own staff. But I did that because I felt I should stand up for what I had been taught. I love the Primary song "Dare to Be Right, Dare to Be True," because with those qualities you can dare to be almost anything you want to be in this society.

In 1980 a Republican party poll in Florida showed that Paula Hawkins could win a United States Senate race, but we decided I had served my time—and that's about what it feels like—and that someone else should be senator. The chairman of the party kept calling my wonderful, long-suffering husband, though, saying, "We need more women in the United States Senate and you can't elect women unless they run. We need Paula to run. We need your wife."

My husband would respond, "You know, that's really true. We do need more women in the Senate, so let's run *your* wife."

In the end, I left the country. I was vice-president of an airline and decided I would get out of town and let the filing date pass so I wouldn't have to run, wouldn't have to answer to that great call to serve. After all, it wasn't a bishop asking me to run. When I came back on the last of May, however, I found out that I was still going to have to run.

There were five men in the Republican primary already, and there were six men on the other side, so I made a crowded field of twelve. We got in the race the first of June, and the rest, as you know, is history. I won the primary two to one and had a runoff which we won three to one. Because Florida is the last state in the union to choose its nominees, we had only four weeks to gear up to win in that general election. Any of you who have been involved in politics know that that's almost impossible. To win, you have to have a lot of people going to work for you very early.

I guess it was a surprise for the whole country that in a state that is Democratic by a two to one margin, Paula Hawkins was elected United States Senator and received 1.8 million votes. We had spent just under one million dollars, so we were very frugal; in fact, we got the most votes again for the least amount of money. President Reagan received 1.9 million votes in Florida, and I must say he had a much larger campaign staff and budget than I did.

I am thrilled, though, that we were able to run that race. It was awfully hard work, required great dedication of our volunteers, and caused my family enormous hardships. But it was a team effort; we ran as a family. I want to tell you that one of the reasons we decided to run was to show that women with families, who believe that no success in life will compensate for failure in the home, can still be public servants, can still be wives and housewives, can still run those many different lives that we all know we live, and can do it well. We have to have role models in this country. British Prime Minister Margaret Thatcher has been a great role model for me, and Mr. Thatcher has been a great role model for Gene.

Gene's really the novelty in this group. He is the first husband of a United States Senator in the history of the Senate. I believe that until men have a great enough sense of self that they are not threatened by anything their wives do, but can see their wives as extensions of themselves and take great pride in them and become true helpmeets, we're not going to have many women with husbands and families elected to office. It can only happen when we have more men who are dedicated to the quality of life in their homes, their families, their communities, their country, and their church. To have that dedication is an enormous burden, and I am very proud to say that my husband is the one who should be getting the accolades in this particular arena of my life.

The novelty of being the first has been an interesting experience for Gene. He went to the wives' luncheon the other day, and he loved the odds. His sister, Nancy Thurman—she's about thirty-six years old and could be Miss South Carolina again tomorrow if she chose to enter—is showing him around Washington. Elizabeth Taylor, Senator Warner's wife, has asked him to roll bandages with her. The name of the Senate Wives' Club had to be changed to the Senate Spouses' Club all because of Gene, but he takes it well and with good spirits. If you saw how pretty those ladies are you'd know why; he's never had so much attention in his life. When I am on the floor of the Senate, where we have been constantly since the beginning of this session, confirming the Cabinet and taking care of the many items of business the Senate has had to conduct, the Democratic members come across the isle and tell me, "My wife said she met your husband and thinks he's wonderful."

One thing I'm discovering as a new senator is that the training received in our schools today is deficient. I'm on the Labor and Human Resources Committee, which is going to investigate the quality of education in the United States. I'm having a lot of trouble, as are many other people, finding employees with the basic skills of reading, writing, arithmetic, and spelling. I think we have neglected these skills far too long to pursue basketweaving or some other glorious thing we have thought we needed. The future of our country is in our hands today. The future is in the hands of the young people. I want to make sure we leave them a legacy that they can handle and a world in which they can choose to lead as well as to follow. It takes great qualities of character to do both and to do them well. It takes great discipline.

Each of us has a role to play in keeping our freedoms alive. Indeed, freedom has never been free. We have to pay the price, and we have to sacrifice for our liberty. We take it for granted. As we have seen our Constitution begin to hang by a thread, I know that sometimes our hearts beat faster and we wonder if this is really serious or if it is something that has been orchestrated all out of perspective. I want to tell you that it is serious. And the issues before us are family issues. There are no men's issues, and there are no women's issues; there are family issues. Inflation is such a burden on the backs of all of us that it is about to crush the family unit as we know it. As more and more of us have to go to work in order to meet the basic needs of a family because of inflation, it astounds me to find people who still feel there are other needs that should be addressed before this one. We have to get this country going on the right track again; we have to get our economy healthy and well; we have to provide jobs for the young and train our youth so they can get their money's worth. If money is going to solve the problems of education, we certainly have spent an awful lot of it, and we need to look carefully at all those programs of the future that are supposed to make America the last best hope of the world.

Another thing I learned early, from my pioneer heritage and from my personal experiences, is that women can make the difference. My husband's mother was widowed when Gene was two years old and his oldest brother was twelve; there were six children under twelve years of age. His father died of a heart attack in 1925, and he had no insurance. What was that young mother to do, with six small children and no training? Talk about reentry of the homemaker into the marketplace. She put those children in a nursery in the daytime, went to secretarial school, became a secretary in 1926, and worked the rest of her adult life running her home and raising those children. That mother developed great souls because of her dedication and her determination to make a success of whatever she was given in life, and she didn't stand in line asking for any help from the government.

My mother was divorced after twenty-five years of marriage. It surprised her children because we didn't know our parents had ever had any disagreements. She had not worked in those twenty-five years, so what, indeed, was she to do back in the forties when this happened. She decided she would sell insurance, since that was where the money was, so she went to school and learned the business. She also taught seminary, taught school part-time, and did other kinds of work as needed to finish providing for the two children who were still at home. These displaced homemakers made a success of their lives, and, again, it was because they had the dedication and the determination and the skills to do it and were free to choose. They didn't go on welfare.

I went to college for only three years because the fourth year I decided I would rather major in being Mrs. Hawkins and go back to the South where I was raised. I went to work as a secretary while my husband got a master's degree. Many women my age have had that experience. Gene got the diploma—but I think I got the superior education—and he was able to enter the marketplace with more skills and could make more money because we had worked as a team. Every day I took my little girl across town in Atlanta, left her at the nursery, went to work, picked her up in the evening, and then went home and fixed dinner. I did all those things that have to be done out of economic necessity. I didn't feel unfulfilled as a homemaker; we simply had to have the money to get Gene through school. After he graduated, I decided that I could be full-time homemaker, and that's what I did for many years.

And then I found there was a great void in the community because it needed so many volunteers, and I became a volunteer and worked my way up the chairs of the PTA. I found out when I became involved in cancer volunteer work, the heart fund, the symphony ball, and other similar things that they are just like politics: If you make a good poster, you are going to be chairman next time. And I make a whale of a poster.

All those community skills and all those volunteer hours are very valuable, and I don't want anybody to feel that volunteer service is a frivolous waste of time. It is needed in our communities, it benefits you, and you can list it on your resume as an asset. And if you haven't given any time to your community, you are in the wrong. You need to work in civic pursuits. You need to work in your church. You need to balance your time among family, church, and community because the country needs you and the attention that you have to give it.

Ruskin said that there is not a war in this world nor an injustice but that women are responsible for it, not in that they provoked, but in that they did not hinder. I believe what he said was true. If we are the majority of the population, we can accomplish anything we want to do as long as it is right. And as long as you dare to be true and dare to be right, you are going to dare to be successful.

Gene Hawkins

It is a pleasure to stand before this great assembly of women and to speak for a few moments. I would like to make a comment or two about the correlation of the Church and women, or, let's say, the Church and Paula in her current role. I do not mind telling you that the question of whether Paula should run for the U.S. Senate was a very great decision for our family. This past spring, the spring of 1980, we pondered long and prayed long: should she or shouldn't she? We recognized the great difficulties we would have before the election and, should she be elected, thereafter; we faced all of the minuses and considered the pluses before we made our decision. I want you to know that all of our children participated, we were unified, and I'm proud that we were.

The main reason I became positive about Paula's candidacy had to do with the Church we all love so dearly. I had seen, as you have, the Church defamed by certain ERA activists, and the press was taking some great misunderstandings to the public regarding the Church and women. It disturbed me greatly; it hurt me. I felt, knowing Paula to be a very determined, courageous, talented person, and, above all, not suppressed, that it would be great if the country could know that a Latter-day Saint such as Paula could be elected to the U.S. Senate and could proclaim to any and all who cared to know that she is opposed to the Equal Rights Amendment—not to equal rights, but to the amendment. And she did so boldly whenever she was asked; she was forthright regarding abortion and the other great moral issues that are important to us. As she did these things, many throughout the land came to know that the senator from Florida is Paula Hawkins; that she is a devout Mormon; that she is opposed to abortion, to ERA, and so forth; and that, very apparently, she is not suppressed.

She has only been in office since the fifth of January, but it seems to me that already this unfair image of the Church and its women has begun to change. I have heard this expressed by some important people in important places, and I am truly grateful for my wife and her role in that change. I'm thankful to you for what you stand for, I'm thankful for this conference's theme of choosing, and I hope that we will always choose the right so that we, as a people and as a nation, will be worthy to receive the Lord's choicest blessings.

To Love Our God

Lynn A. McKinlay

> Lynn A. McKinlay recently retired from the faculty at Brigham Young University after twenty-five years with the Department of Communications. Prior to his appointment at BYU, he worked as the producer and program director for KSL-AM radio, the director for KSL-FM and later as a producer for KSL-TV. Brother McKinlay holds a master's degree from Utah State University.
> He has served the Church as a member of the Sunday School General Board, an instructor in the Salt Lake Mission Home, a high councilor, a bishop, and in numerous other positions. In addition, Brother McKinlay has served as the narrator for many Church films, pageants, and programs and has authored several publications.
> He and his wife, Asenath (Ann) Passey McKinlay, are the parents of seven children.

I realize the hour of eight in the morning is a little early to plow deep, but I am going to proceed on the assumption that those of you who possess the energy, the industry, and whatever else it takes to get here this early have come with a desire to dig in. So, in that spirit, I am going to start with the trumpet call of the great lawgiver, Moses.

He gathered the people together and said,

> Hear, therefore, O Israel, and observe to do it; that it may be well with these, and that ye may increase mightily, as the Lord God of thy fathers hath promised thee, in the land that floweth with milk and honey.
> Hear, O Israel: the Lord our God is one Lord.
> And thou shalt love the Lord thy God with all thine heart and with all thy soul and with all thy might.
> And these words which I command thee this day shall be in thine heart:
> And thou shalt teach them diligently unto thy children, and shall talk of them when thou sittest in thine houses, and when thou walkest by the way, and when thou liest down, and when thou risest up. [Deut. 6:3–7]

I am sure if I had been in that group Moses talked to I would have been mightily impressed.

Now I am going to move to another incident, which took place in the time of the Master and is recorded in Mark, chapter 12, verses 28-31:

> And one of the scribes came, and having heard them reasoning together, and perceiving that he had answered them well, asked him, Which is the first commandment of all?
> And Jesus answered him, The first of all the commandments is, Hear, O Israel; the Lord our God is one Lord;
> And thou shalt love the Lord thy God with all thy heart and with all thy soul, and with all thy mind and with all thy strength; this is the first commandment.

Shall we take another account from Luke, chapter 10, verses 25-28?

> And, behold, a certain lawyer stood up, and tempted him saying, Master, what shall I do to inherit eternal life?
> He said unto him, what is written in the law? How readest thou?
> And he answering said, thou shalt love the Lord thy God with all thy heart, and with all thy soul and with all thy strength and with all thy mind; and thy neighbor as thyself.
> And he said unto him, Thou hast answered right: this do and thou shalt live.

In all three of these accounts there is a commandment that we should love. Given the various connotations of that word it may seem strange to us that there should be a commandment to love. Some of the connotations suggest that love is yielding, warm, intimate, and spontaneous. The word *commandment* has a different ring in our ears. Perhaps it connotes the formidable, the austere, the dictatorial, even the coercive. And yet, as Latter-day Saints, we have been drilled and trained from our infancy that the first really great personal principle God is concerned with so far as we are concerned is agency. He goes to great lengths to explain and protect the principle of agency in us.

Another old saw I have heard all my life, and I suppose most of you have, is that one cannot legislate morality. Have you heard that one? You can't pass a law about morality and expect that it will be obeyed in spirit and in truth. Morality must be engendered internally. There must be a conversion to it from within, and I would suggest to you that the same thing applies to love.

Love, whatever else it may be, must include the feelings of the heart in order to be satisfying to us. Now, commandments don't necessarily conjure up in the modern mind the feelings of the heart. Therefore, we need somehow to work this around so that we can feel spontaneous about this commandment to love and not feel as if we are being coerced. Perhaps some of our difficulty, as I have suggested, is a language problem. Part may also be in insufficient truthful information. I am going to discuss the latter and unfold a few ideas that I hope will be challenging to you.

As I have thought this through from a number of different angles, I have concluded that whenever I read the phrase *a commandment of God* I am going to do a little mental turning around and say that a commandment of God is an authoritative instruction to lead me to the blessings of personal fulfillment. May I add a comment on that. Instructions from God, if they were not authoritative but just suggestions—"Here is God; you may love him or you may not"—would not carry enough weight. If he were to merely give us suggestions, we might stand at the judgment bar and say to God, who is our judge, "But you didn't make it emphatic enough. You left us an alternative." God needs to make his commandments emphatic because the matter of whether we love him or not is so decisive and has such a powerful influence upon the judgment. So, may I repeat: Commandments of God perhaps should be considered as authoritative instructions designed to lead us to blessings of personal fulfillment, not to coerce us but to hold out to us an invitation.

The object of our love is to be God. And I suppose in order to inspire the feelings of the heart, the object of our love must be somehow appealing, compelling, and perfect to us. In this world we may want to love beings who are imperfect because we ourselves are imperfect, but when we think of God, we want to think of him as the perfect being in this thing also—in love. There should be a strong appeal and a compelling power in this relationship.

In the Doctrine and Covenants, section 59, verse 4, we have some help: "And they shall be crowned with blessings from above, yea, and with commandments not a few." Now that is unusual terminology. They shall be crowned with commandments? Yes, that is what this revelation says. "They shall be crowned with blessings from above, yea, and with commandments not a few, and with revelations in their time." Why? "That they may be fulfilled upon the land which the Lord their God has given them." So, all the commandments of God are not meant to impose restrictions upon us or to be coercive but to lead us into fulfillments not violating our agency. We don't have to follow the commandment, but it is an authoritative instruction that we are invited to follow to fulfill ourselves. If we can get that point of view, it seems to me that we are in pretty good shape.

Now, I would like to move from that to a consideration of the kind of being God is. He is to be the object of our love. We have concluded that we must see something appealing and compelling about him in order for the feelings of the heart to stir inside us. Some would say this is the most difficult thing of all—to try to comprehend God. I am going to take a line from Charles W. Penrose: "To know God we must know ourselves." This idea is extremely intriguing to me because that begins to take away the remoteness and austerity of God, and it makes me understand that if I am really to comprehend that being whom I have been trained to call Father, I will find in him and in me many commonalities. Brother Penrose continues: "All the personal attributes which are ascribed to God by inspired men, we find in ourselves." Now that is a marvelous idea, and even though it is early in the morning, I am going to ask you to think deeply about this. The question I am asking you to ponder is this: How did we get the characteristics of God in us? Brother Penrose says we have them, and I am asking you how we got them.

Here is one more line from Brother Penrose: "Mormonism does not tend to debase God to the level of man, but to exalt man to the perfection of God" ("Our Relationship to God," *Millennial Star,* vol. 23, p. 180.) There is that word *perfect.* I respond to that word. I like the idea of perfection. This is very reminiscent of the statement of the Prophet Joseph Smith that we find in the King Follett Discourse. He said, "If men do not comprehend the character of God, they do not comprehend themselves" (*Teachings of the Prophet Joseph Smith,* comp. Joseph Fielding Smith [Salt Lake City: Deseret Book Co., 1938], p. 343). If one of the characteristics of God is love, I thereby know that I have the characteristic of love in me. Next I want to know where I got it, how I got it, and how I can develop it.

Pulling the two together—God and man (meaning man and woman)—I am going to read some scriptures and other writings that throw light upon this subject. Some of you may have thought about this before, but if it is new to you, at least my approach to it, I am going to ask you to be patient with me. Do not reject me until I am through. Then, of course, there is no coercion on my part. You have no obligation to believe me. But I am going to give scriptural and authoritative doctrinal background for what I am about to say.

We are used to thinking, perhaps, that God is far-off, remote, incomprehensible, and untouchable, and that there isn't too much personal warmth about him.

I am going to start with Genesis, chapter 1, verse 27, and with this idea of relating God to us: "So God created man in his own image, in the image of God created he him; male and female created he them." I have always thought of God as a man, and I suppose you have too. And yet, how can God, just as a man, create both male and female? How can he create a female in his own image if he is a male? I suppose you have thought about that. Maybe you dismissed the thought as soon as it came.

I would like to take a statement from a little book called the *Compendium.* It was compiled by Franklin D. Richards and James A. Little a number of years ago for use by the missionaries. On page 118 of that volume we read the following: "Man, in his fullness, is a twofold organization—male and female." It takes time for the implication of these statements to sink in, but I want to give you these thoughts and plant the seeds and, if possible, have them germinate inside your bosom because, in my opinion, there is nothing more relevant to our learning to love God with all our heart, might, mind, and soul than these considerations. This is the object of our love. These are the things that generate the feelings of love inside us. "Man in his fullness is a twofold organization—male and female. Either being incapable"—and that's a strong word—"of fulfilling the measure of their creation alone, it requires the union of the two to complete man in the image of God." The word *man* here includes man and woman without the distinctions that are so sharp these days. "It requires the union of the two to complete man in the image of God; for as we have read, he has created male and female in the image of God; therefore [and here is the summary] without the proper union of the sexes man would be less than what God created him" (or what God is—a twofold organization). Do you often think of the feminine component of God? Do you often think that standing beside him to complete his godhood is a woman? Or, if you have wanted to think about it the other way around, do you think of the female being completed by the male? Whichever way you start, it takes the two of them together to make the perfect unit we call God.

Commenting on this subject, Joseph Fielding Smith said: "Speaking of preexistence and the origin of man, the First Presidency (in 1909) said plainly that man, as a spirit, was begotten and born of heavenly parents, and reared to maturity in the eternal mansions of the Father; that man is the 'offspring of Celestial parents,' and that all men and women—all men and women—are in the similitude of the Universal Father and Mother"—and I am going to take that a little bit further in a moment—"and are literally the sons and daughters of Diety" [Relief Society Magazine, December 1970, p. 884]. In *Answers to Gospel Questions* President Smith continued in this vein: "How can we be the offspring of God, how can he be the Father of our spirits, unless we had a mother there and were born? Is it not feasible to believe that female spirits were created in the image of a Mother in Heaven? ([Salt Lake City: Deseret Book, 1957] 3:144.)

Now let's base this upon some scripture. Abraham, chapter 4, verse 27, says, "So the Gods went down to organize man in their own image, in the image of the Gods to form they him, male and female to form they them."

In the Melchizedek Priesthood manual for this year, called *Choose Ye This Day,* the following very provocative questions are asked in relation to this scripture. First, "according to this passage, how many persons performed the work of creation?" That is, when it came time for Adam and Eve to be introduced into the garden, according to this statement in Abraham, how many persons performed the work of creation? One? No. "The Gods," it says, "went down." Next question: "How many individuals resulted from the creation they performed?" Only one—Adam? No, Eve was there too. Next question: "Were they of the same sex?" No. Adam was male and Eve was female. Next question: "In whose image were they created?" It should be obvious to you that Adam was created in the image of his male father and Eve was created in the image of her female mother. Last question: "What then *is* the image of God?" The image of God is twofold—male and female, not just male.

This is reaffirmed by Joseph F. Smith:

> We have come here to be conformed to the likeness of God. He made us in the beginning in his own image and in his own likeness, and he made us male and female. We never could be in the image of

God if we were not both male and female. The woman will not go there [into the presence of God in the Celestial Kingdom] alone, and the man will not go there alone, and claim the exaltation. They may attain a degree of salvation alone, but when they are exalted they will be exalted [together] so that they may be in the image of God, their father. [*Gospel Doctrine,* 5th ed. (Salt Lake City: Deseret Book Co., 1938), p. 276]

Some time ago in our discussion I asked you to think of this question: how did we get, by the process of procreation that we have been discussing, the characteristics of God in us, first as spirit beings and then as mortal beings, so that as we live here in the earth we can truly say that we have in us the capacity to love? Where did we get that trait? How did we get it? Lorenzo Snow gives us the answer: "We were born in the image of God, our Father." Will you do as I do now? As soon as the word *God* is mentioned—our Father in Heaven—immediately place beside him his female counterpart, our Mother in Heaven. The two of them have to be complete. They have to be together. "We are born in the image of God, our Father [and Mother] who begat us like unto Himself [and Herself]. There is the nature of Deity [notice this now] in the composition of our spiritual organization." It is already there. Now, let me reason with you for a moment. Is there the nature of mortality in your bodies and, if so, where did you get it? You got it from your father and mother by being begotten of them. We will not take the time nor is it necessary to go into any detail this morning about the biological processes of procreation. Suffice it to say that the living seed of the male and the living seed of the female become the nucleus of the new body and that new body carries with it the characteristics of both the father and the mother. We have all the qualities and the potential of our parents inside us because we were begotten and born this way. Now, Joseph F. Smith, Lorenzo Snow, and all the others I have been quoting this morning are implying the same thing. As Lorenzo Snow continues, "In our spiritual birth, our Father [and our Mother] transmitted to us the capabilities, powers and faculties which He [they] possessed, as much so as the child on its mother's bosom possesses, although in an undeveloped state, the faculties, powers and susceptibilities of its parent" (*Latter-day Prophets Speak,* ed. Daniel H. Ludlow [Salt Lake City: Bookcraft, 1951], p. 74).

In the Doctrine and Covenants man is called intelligence, light, and truth. I would like to have you keep those thoughts in mind as we unfold the answer to this question of how we got into our systems the qualities of loving in addition to all the other characteristics of God, and what they are. I am going to read now from the *Writings of Parley P. Pratt:*

"Intelligence and affection,"—and I love the way he put those two together; they really go hand in hand, almost as if he were saying "truth and love"—"like material things, have their origin in eternal uncreated elements." What were the materials of which your spirit body was formed? Spirit substance. Spirit substance, as it was used by our Father and Mother in Heaven to give you your spirit body, had intelligence and affection. Therefore, the elements of your body are charged with intelligence and affection. These two qualities, intelligence and affection or truth and love, are inseparable. Truth, by itself, is austere and dry and cold and hard. Affection, by itself, not founded in the truths of eternal life, could be rather evasive, a little bit slippery. But the two together form the perfect combination. These two "are the foundations of enjoyment, the main-springs of glory and exaltation, and the fountains from which emanate a thousand streams of life, and joy, and gladness; diffused through all worlds and extending to all extent. (*Writings of Parley P. Pratt,* ed. Parker Pratt Robinson [Salt Lake City: Deseret News Press, 1952], p. 48.) These things are pervasive. And if you ever lose either the spontaneous capacity to love or the desire to experience, or if they diminish in you, you become one-sided. If you develop your brain, your mind, and your intellect to the point where affection is neglected, you are lopsided. If you develop affection to the point where you ignore intellect, then again you are lopsided. You need a perfect balance of these. "They are the principle roots from which spring forth innumerable branches, which bud in time, and blossom and ripen in eternity" (*Writings,* p. 48). The elements, then, both spirit elements and physical elements, are filled with the propensities of godliness, including the characteristic of love.

Now let me quote from Orson Pratt in *The Seer*: "Love should be the predominant ruling principle in all family governments." The Lord starts us out pretty well. The basic instinct for most people, although I understand there are some who find this pretty dim in their lives, is to love their families. When a child is born the mother who has carried the child and given birth with the pain that attends this has a natual feeling for her offspring. The father is subdued, even if he has never before found anything to subdue him, when he sees his own offspring lying on the bosom of its mother. One would almost have to be made of stone not to be moved with feelings at that sight. This is what Orson is speaking of. He says, "There is no danger of the different members of a family loving one another too much. They should love one another with all their hearts, and be willing, if required, to lay down their lives for each other. God is love, and He is the great fountain from which the beings of all worlds derive this heavenly attribute; it flows out in infinite streams" (*The Seer,* vol. 1, no. 10 [n.p. 1972?], p. 152).

Now, there is another characteristic of love that perhaps you hadn't thought of yet because we are, in many ways, the product of the culture in which we grow up. Orson Pratt continues, "Love, like all the other gifts of God, can be cultivated and increased, or it can be neglected and diminished: it is subject to the control"—this I want to make clear—"of the other faculties of the mind." Then he makes the explanation that is pertinent to us: "It is not a principle such as is often described in novels, which acts irresistibly." You have heard the phrase "Well, I fell in love and there was nothing I could do about it." To believe that demeans love. Elder Pratt says that love is one of the qualities that should be under our control; "The love which the sexes have for each other is implanted within them by Him who is the God of Love. God controls this attribute of His nature according to wisdom, justice, mercy, and every other attribute which He possesses." Love is just one of them. It is not a device that holds you a prisoner. "He has prescribed laws for the government of His own attributes; and He never suffers himself to love that which is evil or sinful, but always loves that which is good, and virtuous, and upright: so likewise ought man to control his love by the attributes of his nature, according to the laws which God has given, and never permit himself to love anything which is evil, or which God has forbidden" (*The Seer,* p. 152).

Now, there is another quality of love that is interesting. According to Parley P. Pratt, God is not only love but he "is light. God is truth. God is love. [And] the reason why he loves, is because he is light and truth. Or in other words, he loves because he knows" (*Writings,* p. 41). Now this is a tremendous challenge for women today. We are bombarded with the idea that women should become intelligent, that they should develop their minds. I think the authorities of the Church could not agree more with this. Our love is dependent upon our knowledge, and the more we understand and know, the greater and the deeper our love can be, for the two do not, or should not, operate independently of each other. They operate in harmony. God loves because he knows, and in proportion to the extent of his knowledge or intelligence is the extent of his love. So it is in the human mind. "These two principles are the foundations, the fountain of all real happiness" (*Writings,* p. 52).

I should like to quote a statement or two more about the elements of which our bodies are composed. I don't know how you feel about these things, but I have only one thing in this world that I can really depend upon. I hope for food, clothing, shelter, and a position of respect among my fellow men. If all these should depart from me, I am left with me, my body and my consciousness, my mind.

Let me read what Parley says on this and then I will conclude: "Many philosophers and divines have written largely on the immortality of the *soul,* while the *body* and its material connections have been almost entirely neglected or lost sight of, as a mere temporary structure, having no interest in or connection with the life to come . . . man's body is as eternal as his soul, or his spirit . . . it is essential to his perfect organization, . . . both are destined to an eternal union in the life to come" (*Writings,* p. 25). If, as we have said, the characteristics of love and intelligence are in the very cells of my body, I am going to cherish those cells until finally I can rise triumphant in the Resurrection with my body, trained and perfected in the laws of love.

I am going to quote a testament of a non-Latter-day Saint woman. She has an exciting mind and is very highly developed in the arts. Ruth St. Denis, one of the great American dancers, wrote a volume of poems. Among the poems is this: "We are all love beings Groping our blind way toward ecstasy." I don't know whether she is talking of women or men, but I have taken this seriously. This is true of me: "We are all love beings Groping our blind way toward ecstasy." And then, in a poetic way, she hits the nail on the head. This is more literally true for women than for men, but, figuratively, it is true for us too: "We are all Mary Waiting to conceive and bear the Christ-child" ("Eternal Mary" [Boston: Houghton Mifflin, 1932], p. 88).

As I conclude, let me give you a glimpse of what we are intended to be as celestial beings if we develop intelligence and affection as God has instructed us authoritatively: "The celestial male and female, after the resurrection, will be perfected in knowledge and in holiness and in pure affection and love. They will know as God knows; be pure as He is pure, and love as He loves." That is a great thing to shoot for.

Now, my beloved sisters, may I just end with this. It is a divine invitation by a loving God, male and female, extended to me to enter into a love relationship with them wherein fullness of Godhood, a twofold organization—male and female—exists, that children may one day become like the parents. That we may accept the invitation and experience godly love to our fullest satisfaction is my prayer for all of us.

Pornography, Romance, and the Paradox of Freedom

Marilyn Arnold

Dr. Marilyn Arnold is a woman of varied talents and abilities. A lover of the out-of-doors, Professor Arnold makes time for activities such as hiking, skiing and backpacking. She is also well known on Utah tennis courts and has played on several championship basketball teams.

She is a professor of English at Brigham Young University, where she teaches courses in twentieth-century American fiction. She has also distinguished herself as an administrator at BYU and at the University of Wisconsin, where she received her Ph.D.

Dr. Arnold has authored numerous publications, both for professional and Church audiences. She has served on several general Church committees and, until recently, served as a member of the Sunday School General Board.

Last November I gave a Flea Market lecture here at BYU on pornography. That represented the first lengthy and thoughtful consideration I had ever really given to the subject. Then, the planners of this conference asked me to address the subject again and relate it to the conference theme, "Ye are free to choose." Consequently, I have been doing a lot more thinking about it. (Who knows—I may become the resident pornography freak.) But instead of talking simply on pornography per se, I will address a more inclusive category of writing that I will call "problem literature." Within that broader category let me describe two general types: first, literature that offends accepted standards of taste and decency and hence might be called pornographic, and second, literature that generally does not offend accepted standards of decency, but may offend standards of art and taste.

If you can follow me, I want to make one further categorical breakdown in each of those divisions. In the first, the pornographic division, I will identify two types: (1) the cheap pulp novel that trades on sex and violence in order to make a quick buck, and (2) the work of gifted writers who have sold out to the pornographic lure in the name of artistic freedom. In the second major division, that of the non-pornographic but nevertheless problematical, I also want to identify two types: (1) the popular romance escape novel (especially the famous Harlequin romance), and (2) the Utah, or Mormon, romance novel.

We can make an interesting observation about these four kinds of problem literature. One type in each general division makes a perfect blend of content and artistic form, and the other type suffers from a discrepancy between content and artistic form. The hard-core pornography and the Harlequin romance integrate form and content beautifully. That is, in these kinds of literature both form and content are compatibly base; hence, they deserve each other. But in the pornography written by talented writers and in the typical Utah novel (not to be confused with the work of serious Mormon artists), form and content are at odds. In the first, the content is not worthy of the form (in other words, the subject matter is rotten, but the style is superb); in the second, the form is not worthy of the content (in other words, important ideals are stressed, but the writing is bad). What we need, you see, is for gifted writers to produce moral fiction and for nongifted writers to find another means of support. As it stands now, we find garbage being hauled in Mercedes Benzes, and diamonds in coaster wagons. Neither makes for honest literature.

Let's now take up the question of pornographic literature. First, consider the pulp novel. It is generally so stupidly written and so blatantly pornographic that we have no trouble discerning it as trash. It's like buying a bag of steer manure; even if you can't read the label you can tell what you have when you open the bag. Let me give you a quick example from a novel by John Jakes called *The Rebels*. The worst scenes in these books, of course, cannot be read aloud at BYU (at least not by people who value their jobs). Make a mental comparison of this touching little blinding scene, thrown in solely for the thrills of the moment, with the blinding scenes in *King Lear* and *Oedipus Rex,* in which the horror and the blindness are integral to the works. In the latter the language is so elevated by art and poetic convention that the audience is moved and enriched—yes, even uplifted—by watching the suffering of Gloucester and Oedipus through the medium of great art. Here is the Jakes passage:

> [He] went white as Anne shot out her left hand with all her remaining strength, tearing the sharp edge of the glass across his face once, twice—
>
> "Goddamn you for a deceiving whore!" he screamed, knees buckling. He slapped hands over his face. The glass had pierced his left eyeball.
>
> Pink fluid leaked between Rackham's fingers. His slitted right eye began to quiver in involuntary spasm.
>
> Ann started to crawl from the bunk. Rackham was teetering back and forth, cursing and pushing at his ruined eyesocket as if he could somehow stop the leak and bleeding. She ducked as he flailed at her with one arm. She dodged by him, ran—
>
> She almost made it to the unbolted door. The deck tilted sharply. She lurched backwards against Rackham.
>
> The lower half of his face was drenched red. His lips spewed

> unintelligible words. He grappled her around the waist, his spittle and blood running down her arm, her breasts, her belly—
> Making wheezy sounds, Rackham hauled her around the table. Shreds of tissue hung from the hole in the left side of his face. His pulled-down right eye glared with beast's pain as he lifted Anne bodily, started to hurl her away from him toward the stern—
> She dug fingers into his face, felt one slip into the pulpy socket.[1]

You can certainly see here what I mean about a perfect matchup of form and content. Troublesome as this kind of writing is, it is not so troublesome to me as the trend I have seen in recent years among some writers whom I have admired a great deal. Writers have won in this century, especially in the last twenty years, what many have regarded as a great victory for literary freedom. No type of language is forbidden, no subject taboo. The value of such freedom is that it allows an artist to practice restraint based on his own moral convictions. It frees his art to be honest and moral from within itself rather than in answer to sometimes artificial cultural inhibitions. But if that freedom carries no individual standards and expectations of morality, it is not freedom at all. It is simply moral anarchy. Freedom does not mean the dropping of all restraint; it means the exercise of individual rather than collective restraint.

Writers and reviewers alike have hailed this new freedom, and it has been greeted with a flurry of books that have reveled in detailed descriptions of every graceless aspect of human experience. Just look at some of the bestselling serious fiction of recent years, culminating perhaps in that brilliant piece of filth, *The World According to Garp* by John Irving. And look at what has happened to films. We have watched filmmakers deliberately add bedroom scenes and sexual violence simply to win the coveted R rating and thereby achieve box office success. And then we have watched the movie industry tell us that a four-letter word spoken in a moment of terrible stress by an adolescent is more offensive to the public's moral sense than a scene that makes a crass joke of nudity and adultery. The morality of *Ordinary People* is about sixteen notches above that of *Kramer vs. Kramer*, but the former received an R and the latter a PG rating.

In considering what some writers and reviewers are doing in the name of realism and artistic freedom, I think we must distinguish between immediate and ultimate freedom. The exercise of immediate freedom, which simply means the absence of externally imposed restrictions, almost never leads to ultimate freedom, which means the absence of consequences in the form of internal and divine censure. Paradoxically, the exercise of immediate freedom, in the absence of personal and divine restriction, can result in the loss of ultimate freedom. But in spite of what writers do, readers always have freedom to read or to refuse to read. Real freedom lies not simply in making a choice, but in making a moral choice. There is no freedom in choosing moral bondage, in subjecting our minds to explicit descriptions of sex and violence.

I think we must also ask if our newfound freedom in subject matter and technique has made our art better. The *way* a subject is handled is crucial. Willa Cather once said that she could not imagine anything worse than *Romeo and Juliet* rewritten in prose by D. H. Lawrence. She did not deny his skill as a writer; she simply objected to his piling up of what she regarded as tasteless biological details. Could anyone suppose that *Paradise Lost* would have been improved by a detailed description of Adam and Eve's first sexual union? As a matter of fact, can you think of any great piece of literature that would have been improved by the addition of meaningless vulgarity or explicit sex? I don't really believe that literature before the twentieth century suffered very much from the limitations dictated by taste. And most of this century's very best literature works within those limitations without loss of effect or power.

To argue for total freedom from the restrictions imposed by considerations of taste is to assume that all restrictions are bad. What some writers have forgotten is the immense value of understatement, suggestion, image, and symbol. Operating within boundaries, holding back, practicing conscious restraint can release an artistic energy that is dissipated when writers allow their material to ooze out in every direction with nothing to corral its spread. To me, pornography not only is not art, it is actually counter to art. Where is the freedom in playing tennis without a net, or composing music without measures? The real challenge is to illuminate life, even its most violent and intimate aspects, without overstepping the bounds of taste. Shakespeare did it in *Romeo and Juliet*—remember their wedding night? Sophocles did it as he brought the self-blinded Oedipus on stage. Solzhenitsyn did it in his description of old Matryona's death in the crushing jam of two railroad cars. McCullers did it in the terrible fight between Miss Amelia and Marvin Macy. Yeats did it in "Leda and the Swan." The biblical writers who described David's passion did it. Every writer of truly significant literature has done it.

The gap between form and content that I discussed earlier produces a kind of literary schizophrenia in some of our finest talents. Sometimes they write up to their capabilities and produce moral, aesthetically fine literature. Other times, however, instead of being honest about difficult and intimate subjects, these writers get "cute" about them. They invest impressive technical skill in tasteless, often obscene materials. Take, for example, a highly gifted writer like John Updike. He has written some exceptionally fine short stories and poetry, but some of his novels contain obscene and tasteless passages. One of the cleverest, and yet one of the most offensive, of his novels is *A Month of Sundays*. In that novel a licentious minister takes a forced "sabbatical" at a rest farm for psychologically troubled brothers of the cloth. The private Sunday "sermons" he prepares while on leave are brilliant, by far the best parts of the book. But the book also details at great length the protagonist's sexual exploits—past, present, and imagined—as if overstatement were the only acceptable literary mode for the treatment of sexual matters. As a very mild example of the book's overall tone and approach, consider this passage in which the minister introduces himself to his imagined audience:

> I am a conservative dresser. Black, gray, brown let the wearer shine. Though I take care with the knot of my tie, I neglect to polish my shoes. I believe my penis to be of average size. This belief has not been won . . . effortlessly.
>
> My digestion is perversely good, and my other internal units function with the smoothness of subversive cell meetings in a country without government. A translucent wart on my right buttock should some day be removed, and some nights sleep is forestalled by a neuralgic pain in my left arm, just below the shoulder.[2]

To get a feeling for what this kind of introduction announces about a novel and the writer's intentions, imagine *Moby Dick* beginning this way: "Call me Ishmael. I have a translucent wart on my right buttock...." In Updike's novel, the lechery is so detailed and so pervasive that it becomes a great tiresome burden, in spite of Updike's dexterity with language. How many times, after all, in a nonclinical setting, can one smile to hear private body parts named and described; how many times can one endure accounts of the functions of organs?

Part of the problem with such treatment lies in the tone and manner of the narrative style. In *A Month of Sundays* we encounter a very explicit description of the sex act—a senseless attempt by its very nature because no such account can mean the same thing to the viewers as it means to the participants. (It is that gap of understanding between audience and participant that creates pornography. We certainly do not believe that the sex act itself is inherently pornographic.) This particular description is unrepeatable, but I can describe its manner and tone to you. It is told matter-of-factly, smartly, in a cute monotone. It is told in the same manner and with the same suggestion of significance the narrator would employ in a description of the fleas on his dog's back. The same is true in *The World According to Garp* and dozens of other books by talented writers. You can just imagine the scene that describes in blunt, cheerful detail Garp's conception: His mother, a nurse who hates men, nevertheless wants a child, so she uses in the crudest manner imaginable a fatally wounded, scarcely conscious serviceman to accomplish her pregnancy. Literally, in this kind of literature nothing is sacred; nothing is more significant or more worthy than anything else.

Shakespeare, on the other hand, clearly signaled the differences between significant and less significant experience. He used high poetic language to adorn occasions of moment and to describe scenes of love and consternation and grief. And he put that language in the mouths of noble characters. Conversely, to provide comic relief for the groundlings in his audience, he sprinkled his plays with moments of low humor. But these moments are always labeled for what they are, excursions into low comedy. The same is true with "The Miller's Tale" and some of the exchanges among Chaucer's Canterbury pilgrims.

I do not think that a certain amount of good-natured bawdiness, clearly labeled as such, done in rollicking good humor, is very offensive because no one dwells on it or takes it seriously and because the writer does not linger on it and make it the bread and butter of his work. In Shakespeare, the crudities come only from the mouths of the lowbred, and they are always spoken in prose, never accorded the dignity of blank verse. They are acknowledged departures from the norm, counterpointed against the main stuff of the play. Falstaff may be a bit problematical because he is such a prominent character. Remember, however, that even though Prince Hal enjoys Falstaff immensely, the Prince never indulges in the crudities of language that mark Falstaff's speech. Remember, too, that no one—on stage or in the audience—takes Falstaff's banter seriously. And that includes Falstaff himself. Even so, in the end, Hal has to deny his old companion and become his princely self.

It disturbs me to see the creativity of a writer like Updike expended on junk. This same literary schizophrenia plagues Philip Roth, one of our finest talents. He launched his real career with the publication of *Goodbye, Columbus* and several first-rate stories in 1959. He confesses with some embarrassment that as a young writer he "imagined fiction to be something like a religious calling, and literature a kind of sacrament." He adds knowingly that those are views he has "had reason to modify since."[3] It is that kind of unfortunate "modification" that has produced *Portnoy's Complaint* and a whole string of cleverly pornographic books, one of them mockingly called *The Breast*. Since his first work, Roth has apparently discovered the "new freedom," which seems to be interpreted as the freedom to write without any concern for taste. Consider the conflict over religious commitment he presents so movingly in stories like "The Conversion of the Jews" or "Defender of the Faith," or "Eli, the Fanatic." Consider the deep exploration of the problem of exploitation in human relationships in *Goodbye, Columbus,* a book that openly admits the fornication of its central characters without repeatedly rummaging open-eyed through their lovemaking. We can handle the fact of fornication; we all know that it occurs. And we know that it usually has dire consequences, as it does in this novel, because it sidesteps the commitment that makes sexual union meaningful. What we do not need is a play-by-play account of the event.

And a play-by-play account, excuse the pun, is exactly what we get in *Portnoy's Complaint*. We have to ask why he expended his creative energy detailing every experience of self-abuse conceivable for a Jewish boy cowed by a dominant mother and a sexually capable father. The problem of a dominant mother and a frighteningly virile father is surely a real one, but is the masturbation metaphor the most effective way of presenting it?

Clearly, pornography is faddish. Roth and Updike are not the only gifted writers to succumb to its lures. Take E. L. Doctorow, for example, another of the schizophrenics. Who has not heard of *Ragtime?* Few books of our time have been received with such gusto from the reviewers, and we will soon be favored with it in the form of a screenplay. Oh, it is clever, but how often can one laugh at a young man's helpless enslavement to sexual urges he can neither control nor enjoy? Imagine him falling out of a closet in a sexual ecstasy, flopping around on the floor before the astonished eyes of two women engaged in a massage ritual. By way of contrast, I think of an earlier, very moving Doctorow novel called *Welcome to Hard Times,* which almost no one has heard of. It deals with hard frontier realities, but there is no wallowing in pornographic indulgences.

Even the highly respected Saul Bellow has slipped at times into the pornographic mode. And John Gardner, who, in a rather courageous book of essays called *On Moral Fiction,* has spoken eloquently for moral responsibility in fiction, has fallen prey to a mild case of literary schizophrenia. His *Nickel Mountain,* for example, is one of the finest novels, one of the loveliest affirmations of life, America has produced since mid-century. It tells of desertion, pain, sorrow, guilt, insanity, and—the miracle wrought by caring. But in *October Light* a few years later, Gardner cannot resist reproducing a trashy novel verbatim within the structure of his book. And he uses gastrointestinal distress as his major metaphor.

It is useful to compare the somewhat schizophrenic work of writers we have been discussing with that of writers who regularly blend form and content to produce first-rate, moral fiction. Eudora Welty, for example, one of our finest living writers, and one who consistently achieves this blend, has certainly proved, too, that the exercise of taste does not necessarily dictate a mock innocent squeamishness about life and its natural experiences. There is no explicit sex in Welty's work, but she does not ignore the fact that mortals are sexual beings. Perhaps the most openly sexual moment in any of her work occurs in a story called "Moon Lake" in the *Golden Apples* collection. Loch Morrison, a boy scout, rescues the orphan Easter when she falls into the lake at girls' camp and nearly drowns. She is stretched out on a table, and he goes to work administering the old style artificial respiration. As he lunges urgently up and down over her inert body, the youngsters present watch spellbound. But the women present are offended and reflexively want him to stop. They have not made a conscious connection with the sex act, but unconsciously they revolt because the association is there symbolically. And in this moment when a whole camp full of adolescents are forced to confront the reality of death, they are also initiated from their sexual innocence into some vague realization of experience beyond their ken. They have their first tentative overtures into the adult world of procreation. None of this is explained overtly; it is projected by suggestion and by images of mystery that attend the occasion.

That evening as two of the girls pass by the scout's tent in its isolated setting, they inadvertently catch a glimpse of him standing naked in his doorway. If they make a connection between the events of the day and their awareness of his nakedness, they never speak it. The less contemplative of the two girls simply boasts that tomorrow in town she will tell him what a show-off he is, and that ends the scene. But the other girl has been affected in ways she cannot quite comprehend.

Welty has given us a delicate, wondering treatment of a youngster's first awareness of the sexual component in herself and in a boy she knows. This is a difficult matter to present, and Welty handles it with extraordinary grace and wisdom. The work contains no cheap tricks and no ribald guffaws. It is truth cast in a literary form that invokes its capacity for mystery, the furthest thing imaginable from pornography. It says that sex and life and even death are a miracle—cause for celebration and awe, and a breath of terror.

As I suggested earlier, we can protect ourselves quite well from the blatantly pornographic. It is a little more difficult when good writers wrap tasteless materials in skillful rhetoric and serve them up as serious fiction. The problem of discernment is similar when we approach literature that falls into our second general division. The Harlequin romances are not likely to fool us into thinking that they are serious explorations of human experiences. The form is weak and highly formulaic, and thus is a perfect vehicle for the thin and foolish content. On the other hand, the lightweight Utah romance novel is harder to assess because it makes a show of reinforcing our religious beliefs. How can we criticize such novels without seeming to discredit our own faith? Clifton Jolley, in writing about *Saturday's Warrior,* accurately assesses the problem when he notes that there is a big gap in such literature between the message the producers want to convey and the medium of conveyance.[4] The art is too weak to carry an important message, so the message is left hanging on a wobbly artistic frame.

Let's look briefly at the Harlequin romances. If anyone in them ever has a significant human thought, we never hear of it. Most conflicts in these books are clichés with 100 percent predictable outcomes. The plotline almost invariably presents the ordeal and happy conclusion of attractive males and females establishing love relationships. And most often, a female is the central character. (These writers know who their audience is.) Maybe we should ask ourselves if we wish to identify with the heroines of these novels because our own lives are so lacking in romance. Here is a Harlequin romance advertisement that appeared recently in a Sunday newspaper supplement:

> *Harlequin Presents* romance novels are the ultimate in romantic fiction ... the kind of stories you can't put down. These are stories full of the adventures and emotions of love ... full of the hidden turmoil beneath even the most innocent-seeming relationship. Desperate clinging love, emotional conflict, bold lovers, jealous relatives, and romantic imprisonment—you'll find them all in the passionate pages of *Harlequin Presents* romance novels. Let your imagination roam to the far ends of the earth. You'll meet true-to-life people and become intimate with those who live larger-than-life. *Harlequin Presents* romance novels are the kind of books you just can't put down ... the kind of experiences that remain in your dreams long after you've read about them.... There is nothing else on earth quite like the Harlequin romance life.

Here are some of the blurbs on individual books:

> *No Quarter Asked.* All Stacy looked for was a place to sort things out for herself. But the beautiful invalid had not reckoned on the ruggedly handsome Cord Harris, powerful Texas cattle baron.
> *Devil in a Silver Room.* Paul Cassalis, master of the remote French Chateau of Satancourt, desired the quiet, reserved Margo. But love had brought Margo pain once before. Now Paul stands accused of murder. And Margo discovers to her horror that she loves him.[5]

You can see the formula. It is very popular to feature a handicapped person, but never to suggest the possibility that that person might not behave magnificently or might not find a lasting and wonderful love. Such writers almost make us wish for a similar handicap so that we too can behave magnificently and find everlasting love. Sometimes, of course, the object is to produce tears, and so the everlasting lover is killed. Form and content, both worthless, are in perfect harmony.

The chief difference between these romances and Utah romances is the lack of international intrigue and the presence of religious content in the latter. But the trouble is that the religious content is often tacked onto the clichés that make up the story line, and is not integral to the work. These books seldom give us new insights into our experience either as Mormons or as human beings. Nearly everything in them we have heard countless times before. If words were omitted we could fill in the blanks. I opened one of them at random the other day and encountered this typical conversation. It occurs at the close of a visit by the bride's parents to the makeshift apartment of the newlyweds. He is in school; she has a degree in philosophy from Columbia but has chosen to sell Avon products (probably so they can live at a suitable level of poverty while he goes to school). Imagine this scene:

> On their way out, her father said, "Monday morning, I'm setting up a checking account for you two. Let me help until you're through school, and then you can pay me back."
> "No, thanks, we're getting along fine."
> "This is not fine," he said, glancing back. "And I don't like the idea of my daughter walking the streets peddling perfume."
> "I don't want your money. I wasn't interested in it when we got married, and I'm not interested in it now."
> "She's my daughter. I don't want her getting sick because she's not eating right."
> "We're doing all right, but even if we weren't I wouldn't take a dime from you."[6]

Could you have predicted that conversation? When, in this kind of fiction, does the heroic and independent young husband ever accept help from his wife's parents? It's a cliché. The characters are not individuals. They are types whom we don't know as people at all. But we know them very well as types because we have seen them in stories and plays dozens of times.

Even the rebels are entirely predictable. And everyone speaks as if he were imitating a play. Worse still, death and illness and disablement are sometimes gimmicks used to produce pity-on-demand in the reader.

The vehicle is frequently so weak that in its struggle to affirm religious truths without the supporting superstructure of art, it ends up paradoxically telling lies. For example, this literature assumes that it is affirming righteous living when it finally grants every worthy hero and heroine lasting love and happiness. The lie this tells is that virtue is always rewarded tangibly in this life. The good prosper and the evil suffer. This means too that if people are good they can count on finding fulfilling love. Furthermore, this literature assumes that it is doing the Church a service when it shows happy marriages only in those homes in which the wife is a full-time homemaker and both parents are active members of the Church. This suggests, falsely, that not only are Mormons better than other people, but that Church activity and a mother in the home full-time are guarantees of happiness. In addition, this literature assumes that it is providing wholesome entertainment so long as the outward signs of testimony and faith are present. Just as outward show is an undependable gauge of inner conviction in people, so is it in literature. A surface message is not enough, either in our lives or in our literature. And it can often be misleading.

I think this kind of writing is sincerely designed to be good and wholesome. I am sure that the writers do not realize that in trying to support what they regard as the "Church position" they are sidestepping truth. But to sidestep truth is to undermine the moral foundations of the very religion they want to support. Our literature simply must not falsify life in a misguided effort to make us look good. We all know righteous people who have suffered endlessly or who have lived out their lives in loneliness. We know Mormon families who have followed all the "rules" and have still lost children to drugs or parents to depression and suicide. We know that Mormons do not have a corner on goodness or on happy family life or even on religious devotion. We also have to recognize that some of this literature makes its money by exploiting the genuine sufferings of people.

Sometimes, in my midnight madnesses, I'm inclined to blame a book like *Fascinating Womanhood* for promoting a pattern of dishonesty in family life that has carried over into our fiction. The game playing it encourages is acted out in some of our romantic fiction. And it justifies itself on the basis of its good intentions. Take this passage, for example:

> Next time you are angry with your husband, why not try some childlike mannerisms: Stomp your foot, lift your chin high and square your shoulders. Then, if the situation merits it, turn and walk briskly to the door, pause and look back over your shoulder. Or you can put both hands on your hips and open your eyes wide. Or, beat your fists on your husband's chest. Men love this! Or, there is the timid, frustrated manner of pouting, looking woeful or looking with downcast eyes while mumbling under your breath, or putting both

hands to your face, saying "Oh, dear!" These are only a few of the childlike mannerisms you can adopt.

Acquire a list of expressions or words which compliment masculinity, such as "you big, tough brute," or "you stubborn, obstinate man," or "you hairy beast." Other appropriate adjectives are "unyielding, determined, hard-hearted, inflexible, stiff-necked...." Some of these actions may seem unnatural to you at first. If they do, you will have to be an actress to succeed in childlike anger, even if only a ham actress. But remember, you will be launching an acting career which will save you pain, tension, frustration, a damaged relationship, and perhaps even save a marriage. Is any acting career of greater importance?[7]

Note the paradoxical nature of the pretense. The woman is taught to pretend helplessness in order to gain power, to get what she wants, to control another human being.

A shallow form simply cannot carry the message of the restored gospel or any other significant idea. Certainly, the scriptures show us impressively how art enhances the religious idea. To demonstrate how important it is that form and content be worthy of each other, compare the first two verses of chapter 13 of 1 Corinthians as represented in the King James Bible with other versions of the Bible that are designed to clarify the translation. I think that the main reason why we object to some other translations of the Bible is that they remove the art, and without the art, without the poetry, the message falters.

King James

Though I speak with the tongues of men and of angels, and have not charity, I am become as sounding brass, or a tinkling cymbal.
And though I have the gift of prophecy, and understand all mysteries, and all knowledge; and though I have all faith, so that I could remove mountains, and have not charity, I am nothing.

Revised Standard

If I speak in the tongues of men and of angels, but have not love, I am a noisy gong or a clanging cymbal.
And if I have prophetic powers, and understand all mysteries and all knowledge, and if I have all faith, so as to remove mountains, but have not love, I am nothing.

The Living Bible Paraphrased

If I had the gift of being able to speak in other languages without learning them, and could speak in every language there is in all of heaven and earth, but didn't love others, I would only be making a noise.
If I had the gift of prophecy and knew all about what is going to happen in the future, knew everything about everything, but didn't love others, what good would it do? Even if I had the gift of faith so that I could speak to a mountain and make it move, I would still be worth nothing at all without love.

Amplified
If I (can) speak in the tongues of men and (even) of angels, but have not love (that reasoning, intentional, spiritual devotion, such as is inspired by God's love for and in us), I am only a noisy gong or a clanging cymbal.
And if I have prophetic powers—that is, the gift of interpreting the divine will and purpose; and understand all the secret truths and mysteries and possess all knowledge, and if I have (sufficient) faith so that I can remove mountains but have not love (God's love in me) I am nothing—a useless nobody.

We have been talking today about problem literature—the open and the cleverly disguised pornographic, and the popular romance. Essentially, I have simply tried to suggest some things you might consider as you choose books to read and to give away—or as you choose to write. It doesn't take a genius to figure out that the freedom to make mud puddles increases our chances of getting muddy. And likewise, the constant projection of an impossibly romantic ideal diminishes our chances of coming to terms with ourselves as imperfect and still-striving beings.

What this discussion boils down to is this: You are indeed free to choose, but just as important as having the freedom to choose is making a freeing choice. A choice for pornography, though such writing comes as the result of a writer's exercising what he regards as his freedom, is not a freeing choice. Neither is a choice for any literature whose form and content are not equally worthy. Literature that enhances our understanding of what it is to be human, that helps us look with increased compassion on the struggles of our neighbors, that affirms even through our suffering that redemption is real, that testifies to the worth of every living soul, that makes us sink to our knees in wonder and supplication—that literature expands our minds and hearts into realms of freedom that can only be termed miraculous. Conversely, literature that trades on stereotypes and clichés only boxes us all the more securely in the prisons of what we already know and feel. There are no cinder block walls and barbed wire more terrifying than consciously choosing never to confront a new idea, or an old idea in a new way. Nothing is more binding than the fear of a new feeling. Nothing is more spiritually stifling than believing that you have all the answers.

Literature in which art and idea conspire together may jar and jolt us as well as thrill and inspire us. But one thing is certain: such literature frees us because it never leaves us the same as we were. Every blessed encounter, no matter how unsettling, makes us new again. And being made new again is the ultimate in freedom. It is a piece of the Redemption that we may have every day of our lives.

Notes
1. John Jakes, *The Rebels,* American Bicentennial Series, vol. 11 (New York: Pyramid Books, 1975), p. 406.

2. John Updike, *A Month of Sundays* (New York: Alfred A. Knopf, 1975), pp. 8-9.
3. Philip Roth, *Reading Myself and Others* (New York: Farrar, Straus and Giroux, 1975), p. 77.
4. Clifton Jolley, "The Sublime, the Mythic, the Archetypal and the Small," Ph.D. dissertation, Brigham Young University, 1979, pp. 165 ff.
5. *Parade* Magazine, *Salt Lake Tribune,* 1 February 1981.
6. Jack Weyland, *Charly* (Salt Lake City: Deseret Book Co., 1980), p. 56.
7. Helen B. Andelin, *Fascinating Womanhood* (Clovis, Calif.: Pacific Press, 1965), p. 148.

Pure Hearts and Pure Homes

Patricia T. Holland

Patricia Holland received her formal education at Dixie College and at Brigham Young University, where her husband, Jeffrey R. Holland, currently serves as president. While at BYU, she studied elementary education and music. A talented musician, she later pursued her training in voice and piano under the direction of a faculty member from the Juilliard School.

Sister Holland has had numerous opportunities to utilize her teaching and leadership abilities in the Primary, Young Women's and the Relief Society Organizations and has served as president of four ward Relief Societies.

Sister Holland and her husband are the parents of three children.

Two experiences were shared with me recently that I have combined and fictionalized to share with you as a light but important introduction to my remarks this afternoon.

Shattered by the painfully shrill ring of her alarm clock, Jenny stumbled out of bed and toward consciousness. She got dressed in a foggy haze that made her baggy sweat shirt and billowing jeans seem less despicable. Pulling on well-worn Adidas, she padded downstairs and silently crept outside. Moving at a slow, tired lope, she saw the dark outline of neighborhood trees and homes. "I'm crazy," she said to herself. "The whole neighborhood is in bed—where I should be. Why am I doing this?" Then she remembered why. "I'm worse than crazy," she thought. "I'm selfish. I shouldn't be spending this much time on myself. I have so much to do, like those socks. I cannot face those socks! *That's why I'm here.* Why do kids have to wear socks anyway? I haven't lost a pound, but I do sleep better at night. Yes, running definitely helps me sleep better. Probably because no one wears socks to bed.

"PTA, now why do we have to have PTA? Just so we'll have another meeting to go to I suppose. I should go. Someone has to. I'm sure glad children don't go to PTA. That would be five more pairs of socks. But I can't go to PTA tonight and still help with the kids' homework. Now that's ironic, isn't it? I can see the headlines now. PTA reviews flunking families. Jenny Johnson, active PTA member, heads the list!

"We've spent so much money this month; we spend so much money every month. Carolyn told me she had $120 worth of groceries stolen from the glove compartment of her car. This new administration had better make a difference in the economy, but then living off of our year's supply wouldn't be so bad. It would last about a month and guarantee weight loss. I wonder if Cheryl Tiegs eats wheat.

"Oh, oh, I don't think we have any socks in our year's supply. Maybe I should ask to be released from Relief Society. No, I can't do that. I like the society, and I need the relief. I just hope they don't switch me to Cultural Refinement. I just couldn't bring myself to do that Samoan slap dance Diana Davis did while she was waiting for her poi to cook. Maybe those women have too much time to prepare. Don't their kids wear socks?

"I wonder what kind of laundry soap Brad's mother uses. I'm so tired of that kid walking into my house looking like a Clorox ad. I'd like to throw some grape jelly right into her spin cycle. They probably discussed laundry brands in PTA the night I had the flat tire. That was the night my fourteen-year-old told me I looked as if B. F. Goodrich had done my manicure. I just smiled and then ripped up a pair of his socks."

She was home again. Thirty minutes, two and a half miles, clear, cool, clean silence. The quiet was suddenly dispelled by an alarm buzzing upstairs and muffled pandemonium. A few minutes later another alarm and the scampering of little feet. "Mom, didn't you do the laundry yesterday? I'm out of underwear," asked Dave. Underwear. Underwear. She thought the pressure was on socks.

Just then Jamie yelled, "Mom, where are my socks?" Somehow that question was very reassuring—sort of a confirmation of her home management skills.

"Mom, who took my blue sweater?" queried Sue.

"Mom, I can't find my shoes," yelled Steve from his bedroom.

"Honey, can't you take me to work right now so we won't have two cars at Dave's game? Never mind, I'll just have Ted drop me off."

"Ugh! Cracked wheat for breakfast again Mom? I'll bet Cheryl Tiegs doesn't eat cracked wheat. What do you mean the only other menu is boiled, baked, or barbecued stockings? Mom, you're flipping out in your old age! You better stop this early morning jogging."

Given the increasing pressures that we feel almost every day, it is very hard not to feel overwhelmed. We read about Iran and Iraq, about ABSCAM and Afghanistan, of high prices and hostilities and energy problems; and we read about families in trouble. It is about family challenges that I wish to speak, and I especially wish to speak to mothers and mothers to be.

We ask ourselves, "Can it be done? Can we raise a righteous family in an increasingly difficult world?" We search for answers everywhere—in psychology books, in child development courses, and even from Erma

Bombeck. We run ourselves ragged because we want straight A's and straight teeth. We panic that we are doing too much for our children and then get a headache worrying that we're not doing enough. We even get caught in the crunch of choosing between family duties and church callings when both need our loyalty and both need our devotion. We especially feel anxious as our babies grow into teenagers. Sometimes it's hard to see them becoming independent young men and women, and we fear we'll lose those relationships that made us feel so secure when they were in the cradle. And some in our neighborhoods experience these struggles all alone as single parents. And as if these problems weren't enough, we have to face them along with the fact that our hair is graying, our tummies are bulging, and our energies are sagging. Occasionally, we, as parents, would like to run away from home too, but we can't get the keys to the car.

Humor aside, we know how serious our task is. We are, after all, the generation raised on the admonition that no success can compensate for failure in the home. The weight of that statement often seems more than we can bear, but I have come to realize that anything very important is weighty, and difficult. Perhaps the Lord designed it that way so that we would cherish and retain and magnify the treasures that mattered the most. Like the seeker in the parable, we, too, must be willing to go and sell all that we have for those pearls of great price. Our families, along with our testimonies and loyalty to the Lord, are the most prized of all such pearls. I think you'll agree that they are worth some agony and anxiety. To have life go along easily might mislead us in time and leave us ill prepared for eternity.

I also believe that with the task is also given the talent. Like Nephi, I do not believe God will ask us to do anything without preparing the way for us to accomplish it. We are his children, and we must never forget that fact—in joy or in sorrow. And with the additional help we can receive through the veil, we are able to say with the angels, "Is any thing too hard for the Lord?" (See Gen. 18:9-14.)

I have taken great comfort in that scripture over the years. It is, as you may recognize, a family-oriented scripture. It is the scripture at the heart of everything we now call the seed of Abraham, Isaac, and Jacob.

In our early married life, it appeared as if I too, like Sarah, would be barren. My doctor told us there was a good chance we would have no children; but in my heart I felt otherwise, and I remembered Sarah. "Is any thing too hard for the Lord?" No, not if their names are Matt, Mary Alice, and Duffy. Is it too hard to conceive them, or bear them, or nurse them, or comfort them, or teach them, or clothe them, or wait up for them, or be patient with them, or cry over them, or love them? No, not if we remember that these are God's children as well as ours. Not if we remember those maternal stirrings that are, I suppose, the strongest natural affections in the world.

President McKay said once that the nearest thing to Christ's love for mankind is a mother's love for her child. Everything I have felt since June

7, 1966, tells me he was right. When troubles come, and they will, when challenges mount, and they will, when evils abound and you fear for your children's lives, think of the covenant and promise given to Abraham and especially think of Sarah. And with the angels you should ask yourself the question, "Is any thing too hard for the Lord?" If you think circumstances in your life are not ideal, take heart. I'm beginning to wonder if circumstances are ever ideal. Let me use my own life as an example.

Because of various educational opportunities and professional assignments that have come to us, we have moved fourteen times in seventeen years of marriage. When the children started to come, those moves were an increasing concern to me. I worried about the children adjusting and settling in and finding friends. Their emotional safety through our very busy lives has caused me a great, great deal of concern.

When we were in graduate school with two small children, the student housing that we lived in was on the edge of the black community in New Haven. Almost all the other parents in that area either put their children in private schools or jumped district boundaries. But because we couldn't afford a private school and because we felt it dishonest to jump boundaries, Matt was literally the only white boy in his kindergarten class and one of two white children in the entire school.

I can still remember the tears and the terror. This is my firstborn, the treasure of my life. He was the boy on which I had practiced all my child development courses. He was the child I had taught to read before he was three years old, and I was certain he was destined to become one of the legendary greats of western civilization. How could his educational beginnings, his first stirrings from the warmth and protection of the nest be so startling, so much to adjust to. But I remembered then, and I remember now, something George Bernard Shaw once said: "I don't believe in circumstances. The people who get on in this world are the people who get up and look for the circumstances they want, and if they can't find them, make them." (*Mrs. Warren's Profession,* act 2.) Clinging to the hope that maybe this was one of those opportunities for growth, and fighting to control my fears, I threw myself into the PTA. I also volunteered to provide the school's music training once a week. Well that was one year, which seems so very long ago. A great deal happened then and since, but suffice it to say that we are greatly blessed that our whole family has been able to appreciate a broader racial and cultural world. And it goes without saying that Matt has become the most culturally and racially sensitive of all of our children.

Let me share another example from that same period. We were so busy during those years. (Some of you, I'm sure, will relate to this.) We were living in the mission field and that sometimes requires more service than usual. I was called to be Relief Society president and at the same time the Sunday School chorister and a Laurel adviser. I was so worried that these demands were robbing me of close mother/child nurturing with my infant daughter, and for years afterward I believed that every colic or croup in her life somehow stemmed from that period of time. My guilt, real or imagined, was very immense. But with time and perspective, I can see now that because of my concerns I probably worked overtime to compensate for my lack of time. This daughter has now turned into a child with great self-confidence. She is very much at home with herself and with me, and ours is one of the most rewarding mother/daughter relationships I know of.

Our family now faces another very demanding challenge. The role of a university president's life can be a full-time job with a generous amount of overtime. With our home situated on the campus, my children won't have friends living next door, and they will have students pointing them out, nicely, but still conspicuously, reminding them that they are the president's children. In a great many ways the years ahead are going to be very difficult and demanding, but they will carry with them their own special blessings and opportunities too; and I intend to make this a very rich and a very rewarding experience. So it seems to me that Shaw is right. You don't simply yield to circumstances. You shape and use them for your own best purposes. Circumstances are seldom ideal, but our ideals can prevail, especially where they affect home and children.

Of the atmosphere surrounding his childhood, President Spencer W. Kimball writes,

> My wonderful mother's journal records a lifetime of being grateful for the opportunity to serve and of feeling grateful only that she couldn't do more. I smiled when I recently read one entry dated January 16, 1900. She was serving as first counselor in the Relief Society presidency in Thatcher, Arizona, and the presidency went to a sister's home where caring for a sick baby had kept the mother from doing her sewing. Mother took her own sewing machine, a picnic lunch, her baby, and a high chair, and they began work. She wrote that night that they had made four aprons, four pairs of pants and started a shirt for one of the boys. They had to stop at 4:00 and go to a funeral so they didn't get any more work done that day.

I would have been impressed with such an achievement rather than thinking, "Well, that's not much." President Kimball then goes on to say, "That's the kind of home into which I was born. One conducted by a woman who greets service in all of her actions."

Did you know that President Kimball's mother died when he was only eleven when his father was serving as stake president over a horse-and-buggy stake that stretched from St. John's to El Paso? Did you know that President Lee's mother died just following his birth? Did you know that President McKay was only eight years old when he became the man of the house? His father was called on a mission to Great Britain, two older sisters had just recently died, and his mother was expecting another baby. President McKay's father felt he simply could not leave under those circumstances, but his wife said unequivocally that he would go, adding, "Little David and I will manage this household quite nicely." Did you know that Joseph Fielding Smith was born while his father was serving as a member of the Quorum of the Twelve? He was only four years old when his father became a member of the First Presidency. So sisters, if your husbands are called into the bishopric for a few years, perhaps your children will survive the ordeal quite well.

President Heber J. Grant's father died when Heber was only eight days old. His bishop didn't think young Heber would ever amount to anything because he played baseball too much, but his mother knew what only mothers know, and she molded the future of a young prophet. Did you know that Brigham Young spent his very early years helping his father clear timber off new land and cultivate the ground? He remembered logging and driving teams summer and winter, half clad and with insufficient food until his "stomach would ache." When he was fourteen years old his mother died, leaving the numerous domestic responsibilities to the father and the children.

Do you remember that President Joseph F. Smith was born during those terrible Missouri persecutions? When that little boy was only five years old he stood over the coffins of his cruelly murdered father and uncle as they lay in state in the Nauvoo Mansion House. You know the incredible hardships he and his mother faced as they fought their way west, but what you may not remember is that soon after arriving in Utah, Mary Fielding Smith died, leaving young Joseph an orphan. But she had done what no one else could do. Her son would later write of her,

> Oh my God, how I love and cherish true motherhood! Nothing beneath the celestial kingdom can surpass my deathless love for the sweet, true, noble soul who gave me my birth—my own, own mother! She was good! She was pure! She was indeed a Saint! A royal daughter of God. To her I owe my very existence as also my success in life. . . .[1]

Sisters, when we feel the desire to murmur, when we ask for more means, or more time, or more psychology, or more energy, or even when we wish we just didn't have to do it alone, let's pause and ask one more time, "Is any thing too hard for the Lord?" If a daughter misses one segment in ballet training, perhaps the sun will still shine tomorrow. Had Mary Fielding Smith overheard our contemporary complaints while administering to her stricken oxen and raising it from the dead, she might have smiled just a little at our dismay over such things as the price of gasoline. If we seem to lack something found in the homes of our prophets, maybe what we've suffered is not too much affliction but too little. Could it be that the answers are only to be found on our knees as our prophets were required to do while waiting patiently on the Lord?

Now I know that we don't live in the same world with the same challenges our grandmothers or great-grandmothers faced. As the world changes, ours seem to be newer and more complex, if not necessarily more heartrending, challenges. However, I am convinced that we will fail in our responsibilities if we don't exert the same kind of faith they had. An early morning run might help us face a laundry crisis, but Christian commandments are necessary for real salvation, both emotional and eternal. Our prayers, for one thing, have got to be more earnest and longing, as were our ancestral mothers', if we are to obtain the salvation for which we seek.

Now perhaps some of you are saying, "But I am praying now; I am faithfully on my knees, and the answers still don't come." All I can say is that the Lord's counsel seems to be to ask more, however faithfully you are now praying. Are our hands blotchy, as President Kimball says, from knocking at heaven's door? Do we labor in the spirit in any sense that is really labor? I think we, as women, can appreciate that word *labor* in a way that no man ever can. Do we labor spiritually to deliver our children from evil to the degree that we labored to bring them into the world? Is that fair to ask? But is it faithful not to ask? Alma labored much in the spirit, wrestling with God in mighty prayer in an attempt to convince him to pour out his spirit upon the people. We must do at least as much to call down the spirit into our homes and into the lives of our children. Indeed, this very son, Alma, is a living example of a child who was not only brought to repentance of his former sins but who was raised up to become one of the Book of Mormon's greatest prophets. All of this was the result of the faith and prayers of a righteous father. When the angel appeared to Alma the Younger and the sons of Mosiah, he said, "The Lord hath heard the prayers of his people, and the prayers of his servant, Alma, who is thy father; for he has prayed with much faith concerning thee, . . . For this purpose have I come to convince thee of the power and authority of God, that the prayers of his servants might be answered according to their faith." (Alma 27:14.)

I believe with all my heart that the prayer of faith is heard, is efficacious, and is answered. I especially believe that to be true when we are praying for others and never more true than when we are praying for our family and children.

Faithful scripture study seems to be another oft-cited yet overlooked habit, but I have personally taken very great comfort from this passing comment from President Kimball, who says of his beloved Camilla, "I think of the spirit of revelation that my own dear wife invites into our home because of the hours she has spent every year of our married life in studying the scriptures, so that she can be prepared to teach the principles of the gospel."[2]

Where should we turn when we hear so many confusing voices trying to define our role as mothers in today's world? Are we studying the illuminating truths of the past, the words for which prophets have died and angels have flown? Can we disregard them—a rich resource of God's clearest instructions to us—and still cry that he has left us alone in a wicked and worrisome world? We should be in the scriptures, as was ancient Israel, both day and night, and then our problems and perplexities will be aided by the spirit of revelation. And so with simple, traditional, tried and true principles such as earnest prayer, serious scripture study, devoted fasting, compassionate service, and patient forebearance, the blessings of heaven distill upon us even to include the personal manifestation of the Son of God himself. May I close with these two thoughts. The first is from President Harold B. Lee, who said, "If we will live worthy, then the Lord will guide us by personal appearance, or by His actual voice, or by His voice coming into our mind, or by impressions upon our heart and our soul."[3] And President McKay has said, "Pure hearts in a pure home are always in whispering distance of heaven."[4]

I was raised in a pure home by people with pure hearts, and for me that has made all the difference. When my mother was carrying me, my family lived in a tent while my father sought work during the war. Shortly after I was conceived, my mother became very ill and threatened to miscarry. The doctor, whose office was sixty miles away, told her if she were to keep the baby she would have to go to bed and stay there the entire nine months. She, without complaining, tells of the hardship of trying to keep small, active boys entertained in a tent, which was extremely hot in the summer and cold in the winter, while she lay flat on her back in bed. All of her friends and neighbors counseled her to get up and lose the baby naturally because it would probably be deformed anyway. But my mother has a pure heart. In answer to prayer she had a little private inspiration that let her know that she could and would carry this child. She, who has taught me something about prayer, personal sacrifice, endurance, and deep faith, persevered. I thank her in front of all of you for her devotion to and reverence for life. Much of what I feel about motherhood and family I inherited from this saintly woman, and in more than the clichéd, standard way, I acknowledge that I owe my life to her.

May I leave my humble testimony with you, sisters, that there are answers to all of our anxieties. Some of them may come painfully and some of them may come very, very slowly, but I believe with all my heart they will come if we will believe and follow our Lord Jesus Christ. Of his divinity I bear witness, in the name of Jesus Christ. Amen.

Notes

1. Don Cecil Corbett, *Mary Fielding Smith Daughter of Britain* (Salt Lake City: Deseret Book Co., 1966), p. 268.
2. Spencer W. Kimball, *Woman* (Salt Lake City: Deseret Book Co., 1979), p. 1.
3. Harold B. Lee, *Stand Ye In Holy Places* (Salt Lake City: Deseret Book Co.), p. 144.
4. David O. McKay, *Sentence Sermons* (Salt Lake City: Deseret Book Co., 1978), p. 91.

Sight and Insight:
Mormon Women and Poetry

Elouise Bell
Sally H. Barlow
Carol Lynn Pearson
Vernice Wineera Pere

    Elouise Bell is well known in the Church for her talent as an author and poet. Her works have been published in Church magazines and in other local and regional periodicals. She recently edited a book titled Shall I Ever Forget This Day? *which contains excerpts from the diaries of Carol Lynn Pearson and which offers suggestions to individuals in their individual journal-keeping efforts.*
    She is an assistant professor of English at Brigham Young University and has also taught at the University of Arizona and the University of Massachusetts. She holds a bachelor's degree in English and journalism from the University of Arizona and a master's degree in English from BYU.
    Sister Bell served a mission to France and Belgium and was a member of the Young Women General Board for five years.

    One of the most well-known poets in the Church, Carol Lynn Pearson is also an author, playwright, and actress. Her training in the theatre is evident from the dynamic manner in which she reads her poetry. She received her bachelor's and master's degrees from BYU in drama where she twice received the Outstanding Actress of the Year Award.
    Since that time, Sister Pearson has been more involved in the writing of plays and screenplays as well as several volumes of verse that have received wide exposure within the LDS Community. She is the mother of four children.

    A counseling psychologist by profession, Dr. Sally H. Barlow is a member of the Brigham Young University Counseling Center staff and an assistant professor of psychology. In addition to her counseling load and her teaching responsibilities in the Psychology Department, she regularly teaches a course in Women's Studies. Her sensitivity and insight into the human experience is apparent not only in her professional work, but also through her poetry.
    Dr. Barlow graduated from the University of Utah where she received her undergraduate, master of social work and doctor of philosophy degrees. She was a counseling intern at that institution prior to her appointment at BYU. Dr. Barlow has published professional works and was recently asked to present a paper at the Third International Congress of Family Therapy in Tel Aviv, Israel.

Outstanding in many forms of the cultural arts, Vernice Pere is currently the public relations manager for the Polynesian Cultural Center in Laie, Hawaii. Her poetry and artwork has appeared in many Pacific publications and in various Church-related periodicals. She has received several awards for her poetry and printmaking, and last year was the recipient of the poetry prize at the prestigious South Pacific Festival of Arts.

Sister Pere received a bachelor's degree in English from Brigham Young University-Hawaii, and subsequently taught creative writing and English classes at that institution. She is the mother of seven children and currently serves as the cultural specialist on the stake activities committee, as a gospel doctrine teacher, and as a Relief Society spiritual living teacher.

Introduction

The following poems were originally read at a session titled: "Do Good Mormons Make Bad Poets?" It may be worthwhile to spend a few moments considering why in the world anyone would ask that question in the first place, and what does it imply?

To begin with, good poets are gifted with sight and with insight. Sight, or perception, is crucial. Art begins in seeing, in looking with great care and precision with an exactness and attention to detail that the ordinary person cannot or will not give to the task. Only then can the insight be meaningful. One critic has written, "Creativity is a matter of seeing what everyone else has seen and thinking what no one else has thought." But the thinking—the insight—is inextricably bound up with the seeing. To put the matter another way, the poet shows us something with greater clarity than we have ever seen it before and then answers the vital question, "So what?"

Now, when we ask the question "Do good Mormons make bad poets?" we are recognizing the fact that frequently people committed to a set of principles or beliefs would like to *skip* the seeing and go straight to the insight. They don't want to show us; they want to *tell* us. Religious followers are not the only ones at fault here: Reams of bad poetry have been written in the name of socialism, democracy, patriotism, the abolition of slavery, and many other causes.

This problem is variously called craft versus content, or form versus substance—*what* you say versus the *way* you say it. A great many bad poets have believed that their verse was good because the idea, the "moral," was good. But it never works that way. W. B. Yeats said it once and for all: "How do you tell the dancer from the dance?"

So one answer to our initial question is that, yes, Mormons, like many others, can and do fall into the trap of writing pleasant little truisms, or "lessons," in verse that is devoid of any poetic merit. Because we are by training and perhaps by nature great proselytizers, we may be especially susceptible to this fault.

But it need not be so. The *second* answer to the question is, "No, good

Mormons make *good* poets—and here are some examples."

As we look at the specific selections, there is no denying that content, substance, or *what* the poets are saying dominates these poems. The themes are not hidden or elusive. The fleeting superficiality of mortal pangs ("Real Tears"), the necessity of pain in bringing forth joy ("The Pearl," "Twin Birth"), the linking of life from parent to child and generation to generation ("My Mother Called Me Sweetheart")—these themes are strongly sounded and would almost certainly recur in any group of Mormon poems we would examine. Compensation, the balancing of the scales in an eternal perspective, is yet another strongly felt Mormon impulse present in these poems, as witness "The People of Mormon." Indeed, if any single trait can be pointed out as a generic weakness in Mormon poetry, it is perhaps this tendency to want eveything neatly tied up and every puzzle answered in each poem. (I cherish the bishop who told a somewhat overzealous returned missionary: "The Lord may have all the answers, but *you* don't!") Maybe that is why Vernice Pere's bicultural poems come as such a refreshing zephyr: She at least has the widened perspective that resists any temptation to a single culture's easy cliché. "The Visit" exemplifies this restraint nicely, ending as it does in rage and not in composed resignation or resolution.

I rejoice in the diversity of styles and forms represented herein, from Carol Lynn Pearson's well-known epigrams to Sally Barlow's rich, intriguing sonnets, to the disciplined open forms of Vernice Pere. We would not confuse one woman's voice with another's. The stamp of individuality is clear. Each one's personhood is the major motif; their "Mormonness" is developed *within* that motif, which I believe is as it should be.

As I have taught poetry writing at Brigham Young University over the years, but especially in recent semesters, I have delighted to come across, here and there (always, of course, a rarity), a number of such unique voices. I think we will hear more and more from Mormon women who can sing to us songs rich in sight, and in insight.

Elouise Bell

When Laughter Lingers

When laughter lingers childless, born of dusks
you sweeten sense, suspend my disbelief,
shed hate like shadows of stale summer husks,
and tender me to loss in love's relief.
Hope, in her impenetrable designs,
pulls from my recesses a source so fierce,
secures my slight parameters, resigns
my pain, applies her poultice warmths that pierce,

dismisses Time's staunch prophetess from me,
expiates experience, belies shame,
released to Someone's vague eternity,
revives my crippled soul when love went lame;
When all of life comes crushing like a press
I can with hope come home again say yes.

Sally H. Barlow

My Mother Called Me Sweetheart

My mother called me sweetheart, each name laced
with velvet sounds, in wrapped safe-keeping,
suffocating moist against my face—
sucked me sideways into arms for weeping;
My mother chased off night, laughed outloud
at dark who fled challenged in chagrin,
caught me in her glances mostly proud—
made spaces in her warmth for me to lie in;
My mother, putting self as always last
looked long enough to know, decreased her needs,
enfolded me in all her futures, passed
on her middle name, my pain, her seeds;
Who knew when lost and strange and darkly wild
I would return at last her mother's child.

Sally H. Barlow

I Cannot Love You More Than Summer

I cannot love you more than summer; still
when summer shifts and sucks the grasses dry
it burns my memory blank with ashen, 'til
brittle love sifts from this empty sky.
Nor winter, so remarkably benign
bears any hope dressed in shallow air
to wrap me in a season more resigned,
creased in winter's face with weathered care.
A constant friend—not this spring or fall,
each a nexus, a season's interim,
can cement this year, can count at all
as these months move lifeless 'round again.

I cannot love you more than life and still
I cannot love you less against my will.

Sally H. Barlow

The People of Mormon

"And now I finish my record
concerning the destruction of my people, the Nephites."

What did it take to write those stark words,
not fleetingly rapped out on a machine,
nor smoothly spread over a page with gliding pen,
But slowly engraved, a labor of grief,
    Each minute blow that dented the gold
    A spear in the heart of this soldier.

How his cry rings out, through the final pages:
    "Knowing it to be the last struggle of my people. . . ."
    "And it came to pass that my people,
        with their wives and their children
        did behold the armies of the Lamanites
        marching towards them. . . ."
    "They did fall upon my people. . . ."
    "Then ten thousand of my people . . . were hewn down."
    "And my soul was rent with anguish
        because of the slain of my people."

In the end it was genocide.
A people swept from the earth,
    Without monuments or hallowed battlefields.
No medals for this fallen warrior, then,
No Veterans Association, no First Battalion reunions
    To gather annually for eulogies
    and toasts lifted to the terrible, glorious campaigns
        gone by.
No school children memorizing the date of the Battle of
    Cumorah,
No patriotic poems learned by heart,
    immortalizing that land of rivers and fountains
    where Lamah and his ten thousand fell,
    where Gilgal and his ten thousand lay.
No idolizing junior officers left
    to name tiny, fuzzy-headed sons in arms

after the legendary General Mormon.
Well, medals and monuments would have been
   so much ballast to Mormon, anyway.
But his people—altogether another matter.
The chain broken, and
The fervent Witness
    ("Therefore I was visited of the Lord,
   And tasted and knew of the goodness of Jesus.")
Without a people.

Without a people?
Well, not
exactly, not
quite.

When incredulous upstate skeptics
spat a nickname
slap in the faces
of the farmer-Witnesses
   sowers of seed, pushers of plow-shares,
they conscripted for all Time
an army for the General.

In the mouths of five generations
his name has branded trail and temple,
battalion and choir,
scholarly society and missionary ministry.

Out of apocalypse his name
cascaded.

"Who shall declare his
generation?"
Who shall
not?

Elouise Bell

Real Tears

When I played Joan of Arc
I cried real tears.

"Help me, Joan,"
Said the Bishop of Beauvais,
"I do not wish to burn you!"

That's when the tears would come,
Real tears on cue,
Every night for four nights.

When we struck the set
I saw them,
Little dry drops on the black canvas.
Strange, I couldn't feel a thing now,
But there they were.

I believe it will be
A little like that
When the current show closes.
When the set is struck
And the costumes cleared away,
I may drop by with a friend and say,

"Look—when I was playing Carol Lynn,
Back in space and in years,
There is the spot,
The very spot,
Where I cried real tears."

Carol Lynn Pearson

The Pearl

The little grain of sand
Is planted,
And an ancient urge
Begins its work.

I, the unhappy oyster,
Settle in the sea and curl
Defensive lustre after lustre
Around the pain—
Reluctantly
Pregnant with pearl.

Carol Lynn Pearson

Alone

This is how I will die—
Alone
Like I am alone here on the beach.
Those who love me will stand back
Out of the wind
While I catch the current
That rarely takes more than
One at a time
And go.

I will come here every now and then.
I will stand on this spot.
Silent, blown.
I will practice being alone.

Carol Lynn Pearson

Twin Birth

It is the entering, finally, into
the valley of the shadow.
It is feeling its presence, tangible,
knowing the hour has come
and facing
the inevitability of it.
The child will be born, and there
is no way to arrest that fact.
There is no easy ending
of the process begun, often obliviously,
nine months before,
for life, once gifted, demands
the woman's entering that deep canyon,
that long valley of shadow,
that hour of timelessness,
heaven arrested,
and enter it alone.

And at the end of it,
emerging as if from a tunnel,
her child anchored to her
as he has always been,

she sees, suddenly,
the light of the new day,
and everything appears about her
in sharper focus, with a clarity
beyond the worn and faded.
Time moves once more, and she
measures its passing
as if ordering it herself.
Each touch upon her
is an announcement of life,
—of being gloriously alive
and exultant in the event.

For it is not only the child's birth,
but the woman's.
It is that event, oft-repeated,
born of the nearness of death
that separates woman
from the rest of mankind.

Vernice Wineera Pere

The Visit

Silence stretches like years
between us,
the afternoon yawns as
the black leaves glow
in the bowl of your pipe,
their dying smoke
incense in the air.
I have no bright words
that will teach you anything
you don't already know,
and you are past
forgetting the present.
Now, you wear two pairs of socks
on your feet, hoping to cheat
the west wind knocking on the windows.
We wait, and the shadows
gather about us,
stealing softly from the corners
of our contemplative lives.
This island awash

in a great grey ocean
is not much larger
than a sinking ship
and all have gone overboard
except you, Captain still,
determined to command
the last, expected event.
And me.
So we relive the past
together, taking turns
at "I remember whens"
it seems to bring you some joy,
at least you smile, while I
rage inside at the approaching tide
I know as inevitable.

Vernice Wineera Pere

New Bicycle

My daughter rides her new ten speed.
(It was a need beyond all needs,
this blue ten speed).
She rides the road unwinding
with her feet a silver thread
thin as the spokes within
these wiry wheels.
Her head bowed over
the bent metal bar
by which she steers
her way, she stoops
low, her eyes fixed
on the ribbon of road.
The skeletal frame supports
her crouched in the air,
the metal between knees
which pump like pistons
measuring breath
or the beat of her heart.
She is a part
of this blue machine,
an integral part
of the afternoon scene
balanced between

the larger traffic
all of which seems
driven to do her harm.
I am alarmed
at her frailty
perched as she is,
vulnerably,
above those silver wheels;
circles of fortune,
spinning her away
out of my reach,
beyond her teenaged dreams,
and perhaps past the momentum
of even the tenth speed.

Vernice Wineera Pere

Unrighteous Dominion:
A Panel Discussion

Adrian P. Vanmondfrans, Moderator
Brent Barlow
B. Kent Harrison
Carl S. Hawkins
Grethe Ballif Peterson

Adrian Vanmondfrans received his bachelor's and master's degrees from the University of Utah and his doctorate in educational psychology from the University of Wisconsin. His major emphasis in that program was human learning. Dr. Vanmondfrans is the director of the David O. McKay Institute of Education at Brigham Young University. He has taught courses in measurement and research design at BYU and Purdue University. He has authored and coauthored numerous publications in his field and has served as a consultant to several educational organizations.

In addition to serving in many Church positions, Dr. Vanmondfrans was also the Director of Languages for the Language Training Mission at BYU for several years. He is the father of six children.

Dr. Brent Barlow is an associate professor of child development and family relationships at Brigham Young University. He received his Ph.D. from Florida State University and has taught at the University of Wisconsin and Southern Illinois University.

A popular writer and lecturer, Dr. Barlow teaches courses at BYU in marriage relationships. He also authors a regular column for the Deseret News and enjoys writing articles and various other publications on this subject.

He and his wife, Susan Day Barlow, are the parents of six children.

Dr. B. Kent Harrison is a professor of physics and chairman of the Department of Physics and Astronomy at BYU. He graduated from BYU as the class valedictorian and held a National Science Foundation predoctoral fellowship at Princeton where he received his master's and doctoral degrees.

In addition to his technical research interests in physics, Brother Harrison is involved in community affairs and is a strong supporter of the Scouting program. He has functioned in a number of Church callings ranging from teaching and administration to music and missionary work.

Dr. Harrison is married to Janyce Maxfield, and they are the parents of three sons and a daughter.

Holder of the Guy C. Anderson endowed chair, Carl S. Hawkins is a professor of law at the J. Reuben Clark Law School at BYU. Professor Hawkins received his A.B. degree from BYU and his J.D. degree from the Northwestern University of Law. He has authored and coauthored many professional articles and several volumes of legal information.

While teaching at the University of Michigan Law School, Brother Hawkins served as a bishop and stake president. He is currently a counselor in the BYU thirteenth stake presidency.

He and his wife, Nelma J. Hawkins, are the parents of five children.

Grethe Ballif Peterson received her bachelor's degree from Brigham Young University. Her formal education, however, has continued since that time, and she has studied at Radcliffe College, the College of Southern Connecticut, and Harvard University. Sister Peterson is not only appreciative of arts and letters, but she supports them through her service on the Utah Endowment for the Humanities. She has served in many stake and ward Relief Society, Primary, and Young Women positions. She is a former managing editor of Exponent II *and is presently a member of the Young Women General Board.*

Sister Peterson and her husband, Dr. Chase N. Peterson, are the parents of three children.

Kent Harrison: The question of unrighteous dominion is basically the question of how people should treat each other and how they do treat each other. It is axiomatic that how we treat others is strongly affected by how we view them and how we view ourselves. With these points in mind, I would like to discuss the view of men and women that we have from the gospel of Jesus Christ.

Originally, we were intelligences, and we are now distinct individuals. Our individual intelligences or personalities are co-eternal with God, which is important to realize. We are literally spirit children of our Father and Mother in Heaven. We have been encouraged and allowed to come to this earth and have been told that this is a critical step in our progression. We come as little children who, as Moroni puts it, "are whole and are not capable of committing sin." When we reach the age of accountability, then we do become capable of committing sin and, of course, that happens. We desire to return to the presence of our heavenly parents, but we find that we cannot do this without help and that we need help through the atonement of Jesus Christ and through others. Some of us will be able to return; many will not. But even those who do not make it, who do not obtain the fullness of our heavenly parents' glory, will still achieve a kingdom of glory. Those who return to our Father and Mother in Heaven, having fulfilled all the conditions set forth before we came to this earth, will become gods and goddesses, kings and queens, priests and priestesses. Our potential is unlimited.

Our heavenly parents have high hopes for all of us. The instructions we have are, for example, "Be ye therefore perfect, even as your Father which is in heaven is perfect" (Matt. 5:48). There are no qualifications; this is something our heavenly parents hope for each of us. In Moses 1:39 the

Lord says "this is my work and my glory—to bring to pass the immortality and eternal life of man," meaning all of his children. President Jeffrey R. Holland has suggested that perhaps the very first and most significant question asked of us in the premortal existence was whether we wanted to become like our heavenly parents. These gospel principles suggest a positive view of men and women and that our Father and Mother in Heaven clearly expect much of us and have great hope for us. They have gone to enormous efforts to prepare the means by which we can achieve our full potential.

Given this view of mankind, one might think it completely natural for us to treat other people the same way our heavenly parents treat us. However, we do not always find this to be the case, which gives rise to unrighteous dominion. Apparently this message concerning the enormous potential of each of us—male and female—has just not gotten through to some people.

Let me now briefly outline three models of the unrighteously dominating person.

First, there is the person who is openly aggressive or domineering, selfish, and egocentric. He (and I use this pronoun in its generic form) uses authority to gain his own ends. This person either isn't familiar with the gospel's exalted view of man or thinks it doesn't apply to him or to other people.

The second model is the person who outwardly lives the commandments of the gospel, but in private—in the home or the workplace or wherever—exerts unrighteous dominion. This person is something of a hypocrite, with many of the same problems as our man in the first category.

The third category is the person who strives to do right and who believes in this concept of man, but who somehow feels that maybe he needs to help people too much. He may have the opinion that there is too much tendency toward evil in his fellowman, and that they need considerable help. The result is a patronizing or paternalistic attitude. Now contrast that with a positive model based on the fifty-eighth section of the Doctrine and Covenants, which clearly indicates that God has trust in us and that we should have trust in each other as well.

Brent Barlow: I would like to share with you two scriptures, one in the Book of Mormon and one in Paul's writing to the Galatians. Both refer to the divisions we make between each other, between groups. We often feel that some people belong to one group and that others belong to another group, and then we rate or rank one above the other on that basis. In the scriptures we're told that this is a false distinction to make, that within the kingdom, within the Church of Jesus Christ, or among believers of Jesus Christ, there cannot be those false dichotomies.

The first scripture is 2 Nephi 26:33. This is where Nephi says, speaking of the Lord, "he inviteth all to come unto him and partake of his goodness; and he denieth none that come unto him." And then three groups are identified: "black and white, bond and free, male and female." He then goes on to say, "and all are alike unto God, both Jew and Gentile." It seems to me that Nephi was trying to teach us that because we can all come to the Savior and become his disciples these distinctions are of no value. The scripture also seems to suggest that there had been inequities among these three categories (and certainly there have been in our time).

With that thought in mind, turn to Galatians 3:26-29, where Paul makes a similar statement: "For ye are all the children of God by faith in Christ Jesus. [This statement establishes our relationship.] For as many of you as have been baptized unto Christ have put on Christ. There is neither [and again notice these groups] Jew nor Greek, there is neither bond nor free, there is neither male nor female: for ye are all one in Christ Jesus." There is no distinction in the thinking of our Father in Heaven or among the true disciples of Christ.

I think these scriptures have particular bearing on what we are talking about on this panel and in this conference. It seems that throughout history, as far as we have recorded and studied, there has been unrighteous dominion exercised by one group over another. But the scriptures clearly state that as we come into the fold of Christ, those distinctions and discriminations that have existed outside the kingdom can no longer exist.

Grethe Peterson: I would like, first, to talk about the word *dominion*. In the secular world dominion refers to government, leaders, power, authority, and sovereignty. In the Church, we frequently use the word *dominion*. We find it in the temple ceremony and we find it, of course, in Genesis. Dominion is a concept one would assume we understand. It is interesting that the references to dominion in Genesis say that man has dominion over the fish of the sea, the fowl of the air, and so on, but not over people. The other references to dominion, which are found in the temple, have to do with the future. What I would like to suggest is that dominion may not be a legitimate concept in the context of our theology if it implies power, government, and authority, because then it suggests the abuse of power.

Because all the males in the Church may be ordained into the priesthood, some males assume that they are superior to those who do not hold the priesthood, that is, superior to women and children. The priesthood is very often thought of as an extension of maleness, as a primary characteristic, like whiskers. It is something that is automatically male. I would like you to think about that, and I would like to challenge that idea somewhat. That attitude presents real problems for women and children, especially in a family situation, because if a father assumes he is superior because he holds the priesthood then he is going to act in a certain way. And the members of that family will be affected by that.

Unrighteous dominion also refers to the power within the ecclesiastical context that we experience in the Church, through the organization of the Church. If a priesthood leader makes a decision based on prayer and on his own personal revelation that runs contrary to your feelings about a situation, there is a confict and you have to figure out how to deal with that difference. You could be assumed to be unfaithful or not supportive if you didn't go along with the decision. But, on the other hand, each of us has an obligation to receive his or her own personal revelation and personal confirmation. I want to suggest that we do have answers to such conflicts. I hope you will look very closely at section 121 in the Doctrine and Covenants. I am going to read parts of it, and I want to suggest to you a couple of things that I think the Lord is saying here. First of all he is saying, in verse 34, "Behold, there are many called, but few are chosen." The implication seems to be that authority is something that does not come automatically. Further on the distinctions are made even more clearly: "The rights of the priesthood are inseparably connected with the powers of heaven," which can only be controlled by righteousness. This places a personal responsibility upon the recipient of the priesthood. He has the authority, but he has to act in a certain way to validate that authority—to make it functional. The scripture goes on to identify very clearly the human weaknesses that often invalidate the priesthood authority. We cover our sins, we gratify our pride, we have vain ambitions, and then it states very clearly that we "exercise control or dominion or compulsion upon the souls of the children of men"; and whenever this happens, the Lord says very clearly, "in any degree of unrighteousness, behold, the heavens withdraw themselves," and the power is withdrawn. The Lord is very, very clear on this point. Verse 39 is really the clincher because the Lord goes on to say, "We have learned by sad experience that it is the nature and disposition of almost all men, as soon as they get a little authority, as they suppose, they will immediately begin to exercise unrighteous dominion." Finally, the Lord defines the spirit in which the priesthood must be exercised: persuasion, long-suffering, gentleness, meekness, and love unfeigned—or, in other words, after the manner of Christ.

Carl Hawkins: When we read of unrighteous dominion in section 121 of the Doctrine and Covenants, I think most of us infer that there is such a thing as righteous dominion. Whether there is òr not, of course, depends on how we define dominion. If we define dominion in terms of assignment, calling, office, or stewardship, no doubt there can be the righteous exercise of one's calling or stewardship. But if we define dominion in terms of dominant-submissive relationships, I don't think there is any such thing as righteous dominion.

It helps me to think of dominion as being a worldly term and not a part of the Lord's kingdom. Jesus said that rather clearly in the twentieth chapter of Matthew, beginning with verse 25. You may recall that when the mother of two of the disciples was lobbying with Jesus for her sons to have a preferred position, his disciples began contending among themselves about who, indeed, had the preferred position. "But Jesus called them unto him and said, "Ye know that the princes of the Gentiles exercise dominion over them, and they that are great exercise authority upon them. But it shall not be so among you." "Whosoever will be great among you, let him be your minister; And whosoever will be chief among you, let him be your servant: Even as the Son of man came not to be ministered unto, but to minister, and to give his life a ransom for many." (Verses 26-28.)

I don't think it could be stated any plainer that the model of dominant-submissive relationships is the model of the world. That is what the princes of the world do. The Lord says it shall not be so in his kingdom. In his kingdom, anybody who has a position or a calling is called to serve. No calling in the Lord's kingdom gives anyone any right to exercise any kind of domination or compulsion over other people. When our minds slip into the other way of thinking, we are slipping from the godly model back into the secular or worldly model of what authority and dominion is all about.

Adrian Vanmondfrans: It might be useful to talk for a moment about what the exercise of dominion or authority or power might look like in ways that are separate from, but may be involved in, the calling. A person has a calling; that's an opportunity to serve. But what do we do within our callings that we might name service but that we intend as dominion or dominance?

Grethe Peterson: I can think of a number of instances. As a mother, I have exercised unrighteous dominion when I have made decisions for my children that they should have made. Often in a calling, whether it be in the home or anywhere else, the process of allowing someone to reach a decision by working through the problem is difficult and painful. We feel it takes too long, so we want to short-circuit the process and make the decision for the person. Often we end up regretting having done so because the decision we imposed wasn't the right one.

Kent Harrison: One of the key things to keep in mind here is the Golden Rule. If we are working with anyone in any kind of a relationship, we need to do everything we can to understand their point of view. Even if it is a case where we have authority over that peson, it still behooves us to consider their likes and needs and potential before taking any unauthorized or even righteous step.

Adrian Vanmondfrans: Would it be inappropriate to say to somebody who asks why you have asked them to do something, "Because I said so"?

Carl Hawkins: Perhaps I could offer another scriptural model. Grethe suggested that the Savior be our model of how authority ought to be exercised. In John 15, verse 15, Jesus says to his disciples, on the occasion of the Last Supper, "Henceforth I call you not servants; for the servant knoweth not what his lord doeth: but I have called you friends; for all things that I have heard of my Father I have made known unto you." In effect he is saying to his disciples, "I don't want some kind of a horizontal, dominant-submissive relationship with you. I won't call you my servants because servants don't know what the master wants to do." "Because I say so" is not the kind of response Jesus would give because he wants his disciples to share wtih him—responsibility, knowledge, intelligence—and to be motivated by those shared goals. I think that is the form all of our relationships should take.

Brent Barlow: I would like to talk for a moment about responding to something just because it is a commandment. In section 58 of the Doctrine and Covenants I have found something very significant to me because I have often found myself doing things within the Church because they are commandments. After I came to understand some of the principles taught in this section, I changed how I relate to those who preside over me or who may give commandments. The Lord says:

> It is not meet that I should command in all things; for he that is compelled in all things, the same is a slothful and not a wise servant; wherefore he receiveth no reward.
> Verily I say, men [and I assume he is including women] should be anxiously engaged in a good cause, and do many things of their own free will, and bring to pass much righteousness;
> For the power is in them, wherein they are agents unto themselves. And inasmuch as men do good they shall in nowise lose their reward.
> But he that doeth not anything until he is commanded, and receiveth a commandment with a doubtful heart, and keepeth it with slothfulness, the same is damned. [Verses 26–29]

That is very strong language, and it says something to me about two principles: the first having to do with giving a commandment unrighteously, and the second having to do with living those commandments for no other reason than because they are commandments.

Grethe Peterson: May I ask you a question Brent? I am wondering what you do if you feel that unrighteous dominion is being exerted by one holding a position of responsibility. What kinds of things do you do to resolve the problem?

Brent Barlow: I have never been involved in a situation with a priesthood leader where unrighteous dominion has been exercised, but there have been one or two situations where, when I was asked to do things within a given organization by the priesthood leader, I felt the call was unjust. I simply followed Matthew 18, verse 15, where the Lord says that if we have a confrontation or a difference of opinion that results in bad feelings, we should go to that person. I could have gotten mad and said something to my wife or to the home teachers, but in these cases the issue was really between the branch president and me. I simply went to him and said that I could not receive this call. Now, this was not unrighteous dominion by design, it was just that his calling created a hardship for my family. So we explained why we were unable to do this particular thing, and he was more than gentle in helping us resolve that conflict.

Adrian Vanmondfrans: Grethe, I once received a priesthood call with which I felt very uncomfortable. After spending a considerable amount of time thinking it through, worrying about it, and fasting and praying, I came to the conclusion that it was not an appropriate call for me. So I went to my priesthood leader, as did Brent, and said to him, "I'm sorry, but I have fasted and prayed for confirmation, and I have received an opposite answer. Are we in a situation where you have received one message and I have received another?" He said, "No, it was more a call of convenience, Brother Vanmondfrans. Your name came to my mind when I was thinking about this, and I said, sure, why not. And so I issued the call, but I don't have any confirmation from the spirit that you should fulfill that call. This upsets me considerably, and I need to get down on my knees and find out more about what I ought to be doing. I'm sorry."

Kent Harrison: On the question of how we handle unrighteous dominion when we see it, Ida Smith talked yesterday about a number of related questions. I asked her how she would suggest such a situation be handled, and she said it should be approached on a feeling level. For example, if a woman is being belittled by her husband in some way, she should go to him with it. It might require some practice with a friend to decide just how to do this, but she should express the concern by saying, "What you're doing makes me feel bad." And she should explain how she feels because of the actions, rather than directly attacking the person. Sister Smith told us of one example where a woman did this and learned that her husband had been completely unaware he was belittling her in public. It was very helpful to him to learn how his wife felt. Feel free to assert yourself gently, Sister Smith advised, as a daughter of God and as one who can ask to be treated as a daughter of God.

Adrian Vanmondfrans: There are some relationships that perhaps are more near and dear to us at various times in our lives. Let's move on to those. Brent, through your training and your own experience you've learned a good deal about the husband and wife relationship. How does unrighteous dominion manifest itself in these relationships?

Brent Barlow: Problems often arise between husbands and wives when either partner chooses not to follow the pattern the Lord has given us in the scriptures. Men are commanded in three different places in the scriptures to love their wives (and I think this applies to women as well): Colossians 3, Ephesians 5, and I Peter 3. And when Moroni talks about charity, which is the pure love of Christ, I think he gives husbands and wives excellent advice on how they should interact with each other. He says that charity is patient, kind, envieth not, is not puffed up, not arrogant, seeketh not his own, is not selfish, is not easily provoked, and thinketh no evil (see Moro. 7:44). All these words suggest something other than men ruling over their wives. As Grethe pointed out, in section 121 of the Doctrine and Covenants, verse 41, we are told that no power or influence ought to be maintained by virtue of the priesthood, and then the Lord gives some characteristics of one who loves in harmony with the pure love of Christ. (Those characteristics are a very different model of masculinity than what we get from Madison Avenue.) Verse 42 says influence is maintained "by kindness, and pure knowledge, which shall greatly enlarge the soul without hypocrisy, and without guile." When you combine these characteristics with the principle taught in verse 43 – that you reprove at times with sharpness when moved on by the Holy Ghost – I think you have the formula for avoiding most marital conflicts.

Adrian Vanmondfrans: Carl, could we have a word or two from you on the relationships between parents and children? You've mentioned putting these on a horizontal, sharing plane rather than on a vertical, domineering plane; but parents traditionally are expected to perform particular vertical roles in relation to their children, aren't they?

Carl Hawkins: That depends on what you mean when you describe the relationship as vertical or horizontal. If we start from the theological premise that we are all spirit children of God and that our children are a special charge or assignment we've been given, then we will realize that they have just as much importance in God's eyes as we do. That makes it hard to maintain the idea of dominance. On the other hand, anybody who has lived through the business of parenting knows there are things you understand better than your children do and there are things you just don't always have the patience to explain to them, so you very often find yourself in the position of exercising a kind of worldly vertical dominion over them.

I think there is even a more serious problem than that, which is the unwitting, patronizing kind of dominion that Kent described. Too often we are so anxious to help our children through periods of struggle and pain and difficulty, to save them from their own mistakes, to save them from the hardship and the agony that come from having to decide and learn on their own, that we try to short-circuit that experience. Also, in the parent-child relationship, we sometimes dominate without realizing we are dominating at all – by such things as our physical size, our commanding bearing, and our greater experience. We have all seen examples of this when a great church leader has problems in his relationships with his children. They have difficulty finding their own place in the sun, having to grow up in the shadow of a great father. I am sure there is no intent to dominate the life of the child in that instance, but the problem is there.

The only answer I can offer is a need for greater sensitivity to the fact that we sometimes dominate when we don't intend to. I have to go back to the proposition that these are spirit children of God; they are our brothers and sisters. The reason we have been given charge over them is that we came first; and that carries with it an assignment, a calling, a responsibility to help them attain their individual potential. This is a very hard ideal to maintain, but I think it is the only true model.

Adrian Vanmondfrans: Grethe, would you expand further on the priesthood leader and his relationships with those he serves?

Grethe Peterson: I appreciate Carl's model of the sharing, horizontal relationship because I feel that that is an exciting relationship when applied to an organizational calling. If you are working with a bishop who is concerned about you as a person, who wants to know your point of view, and who wants as much input as possible on your stewardship or calling, it is a very exciting experience. But what happens when you don't have that kind of relationship? A friend of mine who was the ward Relief Society president found herself in the situation where her bishop took it upon himself, because he was so moved, to call all of the teachers in the Relief Society without consulting her. Well, that was an enormous breach of communication. I think you can look at it in those very elementary terms—the inability to communicate. That may have been due to the complications of that particular stake, or some other unusual circumstance. Nevertheless, that kind of experience is very debilitating for a woman. My friend did not know how to respond. She felt that she could not approach him and express her concerns for fear of being misunderstood or of being considered unfaithful. But as Adrian pointed out, we, as women and men, have the resources for getting direct personal confirmation from the Lord. We have prayer and fasting, and it is possible for us to *know*. We women have that responsibility to be sure we have the confirmation we need so that we can go forth with that power from the Lord to handle the difficult issues we face.

If I may backtrack for a moment, I wanted to suggest, when I was reading to you from section 121, that we are talking about men *and* women. Women are not exempt from exercising unrighteous dominion. Also, I have been aware of situations where I think women have abandoned their responsibilities in the home with the justification that "you hold the priesthood; you make the decisions." They are not fulfilling their responsibilities as daughters of God and as wives and mothers. The woman has a responsibility to make her feelings known and to be all that she is destined to become. There must be equal sharing and equal responsibility.

Adrian Vanmondfrans: I would like to return to our discussion of "because I said so" for a moment. The Lord certainly said to some people, "because I said so," and gave no real reason at the time. Prophets have done what they were commanded to do and only afterwards did they understand why. The question is, is there any room for that sort of answer within the Church or the family?

There is a distinction which is becoming clearer in my mind, and that is the distinction between priesthood and priestcraft. Priesthood is the authority to act for God in conducting God's work his way. We receive our directions by inspiration and revelation, whether directly to us or through other sources (so that we don't have to spend all of our time on our knees and none on our feet). Sometimes the direction is put in a handbook, which is meant as a guide. But if that kind of instruction feels uncomfortable to us in some cases, we had better get on our knees and off our feet until we find out how we really feel about things and what we ought to be doing.

Now when we feel comfortable saying, "I understand through communication from God that this is what ought to be done within this stewardship," I think we are in a position, to some extent, to say, "because I said so." Under conditions other than that we are put in a little different role. We sometimes don't know what is good for another person, and the only way we can, without doubt, do good for people is to do what God would do for them. And we don't know what God would do unless he tells us. So many times we show mercy when we ought to demand justice (or vice versa), and by doing that we damage people, even though we intended to do good for them. Only when we are doing what God would have us do are we exercising his priesthood appropriately.

If, therefore, we do a terrible thing and pretend that what we are doing has God's approval when it hasn't, and we say, "You will do it because I am in a position to bring something that looks like God's condemnation down on you if you don't," that is priestcraft. Whether we do it as parents, as priesthood leaders, or in other roles, if we remove from someone the inclination and the rightful opportunity to disagree with us, unless they stand in a dangerous position, and we do it because of our own whims, then we are not appropriately exercising God's authority. Instead, we are exercising priestcraft.

Carl Hawkins: Let me suggest another distinction in response to this question. I think there is a place for commands without explanations, but even in those situations I don't like the "because I said so" kind of explanation.

The Lord has often given us commands without explanations. But I believe that occurs when the Lord knows we are probably not yet capable of understanding; so explanations would be futile, they wouldn't work, and we wouldn't be capable of handling them. We sometimes face these kinds of situations in our relationships with our children. Our perspective is, at times, broader than our children, not because of superior wisdom, but because we have been around a little longer, we have seen a few things our children haven't seen yet, and we have a little more information. And while some kinds of commands cannot be explained adequately or at least cannot be understood by young people, I think the error we most often make is assuming that they won't understand. And that is a cop-out, an excuse for not giving them as much of the relevant information as we can. We are all a bit too impatient, but I think the only time when it is legitimate to say "because I said so" to our children is when our experience and perspective cannot be adequately explained.

Grethe Peterson: I would like to comment on that too. I think we need to make one other distinction: The ability to say to your children, "do it because I say so," and to have them accept that, is dependent upon enormous trust that has been developed between the child and parent. There is a time when you have to save the child from running into the street, and you want to develop that child's awareness so that when you say come back or stop, the child will stop for his own safety. But that is possible only when there is trust. It seems to me that a relationship of trust in the Lord and in our leaders applies. If the Lord gives these instructions and we trust the priesthood leader who is conveying them, we are able to accept his counsel because of the trust we have developed.

Adrian Vanmondfrans: The panel members will now respond to questions that have been submitted by the audience.

Grethe Peterson: I have a question that addresses the issue of righteous leadership in the home. "What if the woman decides after marriage to opt for a career and her husband thinks that she should center her activities in the home? Does the husband have the right or the duty to say anything?" I think this comes down to what kind of a relationship this husband and wife have and what the level of communication is in their marriage. I cannot imagine living in a situation where there would be any hesitancy on the part of either partner to express his or her point of view on something as important as that. Now, if the man in the family is not willing to negotiate some kind of solution, it seems to me they are in big trouble because this kind of a decision is obviously important to her, and there has to be a solution.

I think this problem is not one for which the gospel provides an easy solution. It is a cultural problem, and more and more women in the Church are facing it. Working outside of the home, in many cases, is not a matter of choice; it is a matter of necessity. Women are having to go to work to be able to send their sons on missions and even to put food on the table. That is reality, and we have to deal with it. I think one of the reasons we sometimes feel that the general leadership of the church isn't quite sensitive enough to what is happening in women's lives is that many of them were raised in a completely different generation. The experience they had of family life and the role of women was very different from what is happening today because the economics of life were different at that time. There is bound to be a gap between their experience and ours today.

But I do think that our General Authorities are making an enormous effort to become informed and that there is greater access now, in some ways, to what is happening to women.

Another question someone asked is, "What about the husband who doesn't discipline the children and forces the wife to take full responsibility?" He is relinquishing his responsibility. Childbearing is a mutual kind of responsibility that a father and mother must share.

Brent Barlow: I think many of us can identify with the statement, "I'm torn between expectations put upon me by church, husband, and self. If I do not accept all that comes to me with a positive attitude, and an attitude of service, I begin to feel that I do not measure up or that I am being selfish. Where do I draw the line between giving to others and thinking of myself? How can I make a clear choice when, if I say no, the guilt feelings override the actual doing of the thing?"

I think all of us in the Church at one time or another feel this way. When we are overwhelmed with responsibility from different sources, whether it be from church, marriage, family, or community, many of us think of the scripture that says, "Be ye therefore perfect." I think we have to look at the context of that scripture. The Savior was talking about being perfect in our love toward other people and being perfect to our Father in Heaven.

When I feel discouraged, I often read Mosiah 4:27, which says, "And see that all these things are done in wisdom and order; for it is not requisite that a man should fun faster than he has strength. And again, it is expedient that he should be diligent, that thereby he might win the prize; therefore, all things must be done in order." This thought, by the way, was also expressed to the Prophet Joseph in section 10 of the Doctrine and Covenants, verse 4, where he was encouraged not to run faster or labor more than he had strength or means, which simply says to me that each of us needs to assess the strength we have. Some things we can do, but some things we can't. We could also learn from Paul's milk and meat analogy. We always think we are ready for the meat while everyone else is still on milk, but I think there are times when we must simply say, "I'm not ready for that, and I can't do it."

I read a statement not long ago by Brigham Young about Matthew 5:48 that radically changes my concept of what the Lord expects. Brigham Young said that if we do as well as we are capable of doing, we are perfect. And he said the curse that will come upon the seed of Adam and Eve will be for not doing all we are capable of doing. I don't have to do something far beyond my capacity if all the Lord is asking, when he asks us to be perfect, is to do all we are capable of doing. However, we should explore what we are capable of doing, for we may be capable of doing more than we think. But, certainly, the Lord does not demand that we do what we are not capable of doing.

Adrian Vanmondfrans: Part of doing things in order means setting appropriate priorities for our various stages in life. There are times when our children must take more of our time than they do at other times. As they grow older, they take a different kind of time—maybe not as many hours, but they begin to require the kind of time and relationship where we can reach more deeply into their mental and spiritual concerns. We need to always allow for these differences in demand.

Kent Harrison: There are several questions here on a similar subject. Let me pick out one and read it: "We are trying to cope on a day-to-day basis with real or imagined prejudices and biases against us as women within the Church. You men on the panel seem to be out of touch with the impact that this has on us. Grethe pointed it out in black and white during her opening remarks. Men in the Church seem unwilling to recognize or deal with many of the problems of women. For example, I cite the Church's handling of recent programs dealing with depression. My question is, how can our needs be met when men have the ultimate power of veto?"

That is a very practical question. We have been rather theoretical here, (and I think one reason for that is we don't know all the answers). The church structure being what it is, we're not in a position to mount a revolution, and yet help like this is needed. I hope, ultimately, that if we talk enough about this problem—to the right audiences—it will sink in. I don't know quite how to solve this problem except by continually trying and pushing. I'd appreciate hearing responses from other members of the panel on that.

Adrian Vanmondfrans: I may have a little different perspective than some, and I may not be able to fully explain it; but let me try. A number of years ago I worried a great deal about the lack of information flowing upward from the Church membership to Church leadership. There is a tendency, when you are in a leadership position, to assume that everything under your stewardship is going well, so if someone above you in the Church hierarchy asks how things are going, you say, "fine." If you are a father, then everything is fine in your family if the home teacher asks. If you are a home teacher, then everything is fine with your families when the priesthood leader asks; and so on up the line. For a long time, having the General Authorities go to stake conferences and talk to stake presidents was the only system the central Church had for obtaining information about what was happening in the Church, other than the standard reports we all submitted. The tendency was to think that things were fine because that was all they heard. And when leaders would discover a small problem, sometimes a whole flood of problems would follow. That was a little bit frightening, so it was easier to believe things were fine.

A number of years ago, however, there were quite a few men and women who had the opportunity to talk with some of the General Authorities about the possibility of opening up more channels of communication going upward as well as downward, and that process slowly started to grow until it became somewhat formalized. I am aware of a number of studies in which comments like the one I read have not only been made, but have been transmitted upward and have been aggregated so that what appears sometimes to be a lone cry of pain out there—"I'm hurting and I need help"—has been magnified and brought together with other cries of pain. There is more and more recognition. The Church leaders are beginning to recognize that there are many problems we need to deal with that we haven't even been aware of. But this is going to take some time.

How many years are we away from the time when General Authorities knew every stake president by his first name? That was only twenty years ago, and now we have so many stake presidents no one could possibly remember all their names. The Church has suddenly grown, and as we've grown the need has magnified for additional ways to get information about and help with the problems we are dealing with in life.

But the most important relationships in your life are the relationships between you and your Savior, you and your immediate family, and you and the servants of the Lord who have been called to try to help you. You ought to feel the most pain if that relationship between you and your Savior isn't right. That is your highest priority. The next highest is the one between you and your family; and if that isn't right, then do something about it. Then you can begin to look at these other relationships.

What I am trying to say is that there are a lot of responsibilities we might want to unload on some organization somewhere that we really shouldn't. We ought to look first at ourselves and our relationship with deity and then at our relationship with those near and dear to us. If in our own homes we are a cause of conflict, how can we imagine that we are justified in saying, "The Church isn't doing anything for me." We are, then, causing our own problems to some extent, and we need to accept at least some responsibility for solving them.

Now I don't mean to say by that that this issue isn't a legitimate concern. We are trying to find out what the legitimate concerns are, but I'm trying to make two points. One is that there is a serious effort on the part of the Church to find out what the problems are and what might be useful solutions from an organizational point of view. But, on the other hand, we have always had the major solution to life's problems, and that is our relationship with our Savior and with our family. That fundamental truth has never changed.

Carl Hawkins: That's an answer I would share in, but at the same time I have to recognize that it has an element of cop-out in it because it says, "Don't complain about the fact that you don't have access to the organizational decision-making process because they don't count as much as these other things." Well, even though it is a cop-out, it is also true. They don't count as much as these other things. I may be getting a little too old and a little too tired, but these *organizational* functions of the priesthood don't really excite me that much any more. I'm ready to turn my time and attention back to the more intimate and personal relationships.

Now, let me read a very profound question that I received. A tremendous amount of thought and sensitivity has gone into this. "I get uncomfortable when leaders of the Church insist that the women of the Church are equal. I feel patronized when I am told that I am just as good as any man. Help me understand my feelings of being dominated by leaders who are telling me that they are not dominating me."

The main thing I can do is react to the question; I'm not really sure I can help with the understanding. Why do you get uncomfortable when leaders of the Church insist that women are equal, and why do you feel you are being patronized? There is still too much of both in the institutional arrangements; and the attitudes of many people in the Church seem to say, "We don't really believe we're all our Heavenly Father's children and of equal value." So you pick up the dissonance between what is being said and what is being done, between what is being said and what is being felt, and you understandably resent that.

"Help me understand my feelings toward leaders who are telling me they are not dominating me." I think anybody who tells you that they are not dominating you is in trouble because people usually say that by way of rationalization. Those kinds of things, it seems to me, don't need to be said if we have the right kinds of working relationships. That is, you don't have to assure people that they are of equal value if you are treating them as people of equal value. You don't have to tell people you are not dominating them if you are *not* dominating them. What you are doing, it seems to me, is reacting to the difference between what we are doing and what we are saying. Even so, there is some value in what we are saying because it may help to raise our consciousness enough so that, bit by bit, we may overcome what is being done.

Talents Bring Joy

Lee Provancha Day

> The daughter of an Air Force officer, Lee Provancha Day was born in Newfoundland, Canada, which proved to be the beginning of her world travels.
> Sister Day graduated from the North Carolina School of the Arts and attended the School of American Ballet. Professionally, Lee danced with the American Ballet Theatre for three years prior to coming to Utah as a principle dancer with Ballet West four years ago. Her talent has captivated audiences in our country as well as abroad.
> She is currently on leave from Ballet West for obvious reasons: she and her husband are expecting their first child.

When I began organizing my thoughts for this talk I thought about the talent for dance with which I have been blessed, and the word *joy* kept coming into my mind. Perhaps this was because I have received so much joy and pleasure from dance, a joy any of us can achieve as we develop our own talents or help our children develop theirs. I believe there are four levels of joy (which are spoken of by Richard M. Eyre in his book *The Discovery of Joy*) that relate to the joy we can receive from developing our talents.

The first consists of the physical and temporal pleasures and experiences of the earth. Some examples might be the joy of work; the joy of choice and self-determination; the joy of health, physical gifts, and talents; and the joy of music, dance, sports, and other activities. In some ways, this level of joy may be the most important because it is a prerequisite for the other three levels.

My mother had a dream: she wanted a girl with blue eyes who could dance, so when I came along and showed an interest in dance, she started me in ballet classes when I was five. At age six I developed leg perthis disease, which affects the hip joint. I was put in the hospital, and while there I received a blessing and because of the unquestioning faith that most children have, I knew everything would be okay. Although the doctors were very unsure of the future, especially when it came to dancing, when I was nine the doctors decided the hip was well enough for me to start walking again and said I should start taking dance classes to rebuild my left leg. They did caution me to not be too disappointed if I weren't able to do very much, but I was determined, and I had a very patient teacher who made me do everything twice on my left leg to build it back up.

Dance has helped me learn a great deal of discipline, not only of body, but of mind. This discipline carries over into my everyday life and is helping me to be more organized. I have also developed a great deal of respect for the human body and how we must learn to care for and nourish it, and then it will repay us by letting us do things we thought were impossible. Dance has also brought me great joy and satisfaction by giving me an outlet, a way to express myself. To feel creative is a wonderful feeling, and it makes me wonder what joy our Savior must have felt as he created us and our beautiful world.

If I had to pick the one way in which dance has helped me the most, it would have to be the realization of my worth as an individual. I know through my talent I have something to offer. I have worked hard and have accomplished something I can be proud of, and that is a very good feeling.

Dance is like anything else. Unless you share it with others, your joy is incomplete. The second level of joy is achieved by adding relationships and achievements. This level includes the joy of family; the joy of communication; the joy of creating, building, and striving for goals; the joy of correct choices; and the joy of being appreciated. The second level of joy not only enriches our own lives by helping us feel appreciated for our talents, but it also gives us the opportunity to communicate with and touch others.

Through dance something of beauty is given to an audience. Not only are the sets and costumes beautiful, but the human body—a creation of God—moves gracefully through space. Over seventy-seven thousand people saw Ballet West's production of *The Nutcracker* this year, and for many of them it was not the first time. They had received joy before and were back to experience it once more.

There are more specific ways we can use our talents as a tool to build up God's kingdom. I was involved in a production of *South Pacific,* produced by the students of the University of Utah stake who donated the proceeds to the Jordan River Temple. Even though it was a lot of hard work for everyone, we received a lot of joy from knowing that we were not only giving immediate pleasure to our audiences but that we were giving a gift that would last beyond when the curtain fell and the theater was empty.

Many times we are able to touch people's lives and we don't even realize it. I received a letter last summer that made me think once again how important it is that we *always* be good examples. The letter read in part:

> Dear Lee,
> In all probability you will not remember me, but I definitely remember you. I met you in Estoril, Portugal, about eight years ago. I was one of the myriad of young people at the ballet school there. I often watched you dance, walk, and talk. Then one day as we were discussing religion you came by. You told us you were a Mormon.

You told us a few things about the Church. I knew very little of the
Church, so I didn't say much.

I'd like to tell you now that my husband and I were sealed in the
Los Angeles Temple on June 24, 1978. I have always said I'd write or
call anyone who had to do with my conversion so that they'd
understand that they plant seeds of the gospel wherever they go.

From this letter I experienced the real meaning of the second level of
joy, the joy of being appreciated. But we can still obtain even greater joy as
we move to the next level, which includes the joy of knowing which priorities are correct, the joy of learning, and the joy of knowing our purpose.
It is through the addition of gospel knowledge and insight that we are
able to achieve this level, and I would like to apply it to the joy we can
obtain by being a professional artist and at the same time being a good
Latter-day Saint.

I want you to know that being a Latter-day Saint and an artist is not
always easy. The environment in which most professional artists work usually is not the best. Mormon artists have to realize this from the beginning,
and hopefully, through their testimonies, they will find the strength they
need to handle any situation.

I made the decision when I graduated from high school that I had to go
to New York, much to the horror of my parents, and I spent the next five
years there until I was twenty-three. These are years of much changing and
questioning for any young person. And yes, I did question. I couldn't
stand here and say that I was a perfect angel all that time. And while I do
have regrets, I can also say that I learned many things in those five years,
probably the most invaluable of which was how important it is to instill in
our children—from a very early age—a desire for righteousness, a strong
feeling for good and evil, and an understanding of the importance of setting goals and striving each day to obtain them. No matter what I went
through I always had an ultimate goal and a plan for my life. The total
picture may have become clouded at times, but there was an inner strength
and knowledge that guided me through the clouds.

Before I ever began my professional career I knew that I wanted to be
married in the temple and to have a family. Dancing was and always will
be a part of my life, but not at the expense of these other things. I didn't
want to find myself like so many dancers I know who reach thirty or
thirty-five alone, with a badly worn body, and with no real plan for the
future. So after five years in New York, I decided I would rather dance in
a smaller company where I would be able to progress more quickly since I
planned to dance for only a few more years. I decided to come to Salt Lake
because I had family close by and because I knew the kind of people I
would find here would have the same desires in life that I had. And yes,
finding a husband was definitely part of the plan. So I joined Ballet West
as a soloist in November of 1976 and was promoted to a principal six
months later.

Before long I met a medical student and we started dating. It didn't take too long before the subject of marriage did come up, and then it became clear that he felt I should be willing to give up my job with Ballet West and to move to wherever he would be doing his internship. I suppose this was when I decided it wasn't true love because I really didn't feel ready to give up my career. I'm glad I made that decision because I did find the right person for me soon after. I am so thankful for my husband, Weston. He recognized my need to dance and has given me so much support and encouragement. We have been married for three years and are expecting our first child in about six weeks. We are very excited and are very anxious for these next few weeks to pass quickly.

I must say the decision to have a child at this time was not an easy one. I have always loved children, and there was never any question that one day I would be a mother. It is just that everything has gone so well for me with my dancing these past few years that it would have been very easy to put off starting our family for a little while longer. It is in making decisions such as these that the insights and knowledge of the gospel can give us direction. My husband and I believe in families, and we realized it was time to get started. We have had three years alone together to develop a strong bond and love as husband and wife, and now we feel the need for that extra love that comes to a marriage blessed through the presence of a precious little spirit. So even though it was hard to stop dancing at this time, I know that the rewards of following our Father in Heaven's plan cannot be questioned.

These first three levels of joy consist of earthly joys, but because of our beliefs we know of a life after this that must be a joyous place. To attain the fourth level we are blessed with the presence of the Holy Ghost, which envelopes all other joy as an atmosphere shrouds an earth, and turns earthly, temporary joys into heavenly, eternal joy. This fourth level is built around the joy of faith and of true, communicating prayer, the joy of the Atonement and of its power to sanctify, and the joy of ultimate confidence in one's self as a son or daughter of God.

It is a great joy to know that we have a Father in Heaven who approves of what we have done with the talents he has given us and who is pleased with the knowledge we have acquired as we have developed our talents. When we acquire this divine knowledge through magnifying our talents, they become ours to keep forever.

I pray that we will not be afraid to excel in whatever field we choose and that we will teach our children well so they will be able to always know what is important. Then they will grow from the choices they make, they will be able to achieve the ultimate level of joy available to all, and they will have peace because they will know their Father in Heaven smiles upon them.

Fortifying Ourselves Against Evil

Carol Ann Hawley

A native of Glendale, California, Carol Ann Hawley transferred to Brigham Young University this year from Glendale College where she served as the student body president and as a member of the school's Board of Trustees. While on the board she sponsored a bill in the state legislature to modify the Community College Code of California. A major in Organizational Communication at BYU, Carol serves as the publicity chairman for the ASBYU Women's Office and is a member of the Women's Board. Last year she was named Lamda Delta Sigma's National Woman of the Year.

Carol loves to sing and enjoys politics. She currently serves on the County Central Committee, Forty-first District, for the State of California.

Have you ever wondered what it would be like if you could trade places with one of your progenitors and live life as they knew it? I have. I am certainly grateful that I was not alive during the time of the pioneers. Dressing up and marching in the Primary's Pioneer Day parade was as close to the real adventure as I would care to come. I am even more grateful that I was not alive during the Depression when people sold apples on the street corners to survive. I sold candy bars to raise money for my junior high school when I was in the ninth grade, and if my existence had depended on my salesmanship I would not have lasted long.

Today we experience many things that our forefathers never knew. For us the battle is not against nature or against poverty and widespread deprivation; in our day we fight a different kind of battle.

When I ask my fellow students what they see as today's problems, they suggest such things as increasing violence, crime rates, and immorality. Then they usually add, "What we really wonder about is what will happen to our children. What kind of world will we be bringing them into?"

I think the Apostle Paul saw our day and the battles we would face when he wrote, "For we wrestle not against flesh and blood but against principalities, against powers, against the rulers of darkness of this world, against spiritual wickedness in high places" (Eph. 6:12). He goes on to tell us to put on the whole armor of God as we fight this battle. The armor of faith and courage will be needed for the battle against sin that will inevitably take place in our communities, in our states, and in our nation.

Today's problems are much like the homework my professors assign me. No matter how long I ignore it, it never seems to go away. Similarly, it seems that anything of worth, especially those ideals to which we are really committed, will die unless it is maintained by sacrifice and service. There are several reasons people give when explaining why they can't serve. I've heard people say, for example, "We have this year's reading assignment in church, and I am too busy reading my scriptures to read anything else." "I don't have time to become involved and informed." Or "The school board has already made its decision about what kind of sex education is going to be part of the curriculum for this year." Or "My senator is so liberal that if I wrote him a letter expressing my views he would just ignore them." Those are all fine excuses, but that is all they are.

We must be willing to sacrifice if we are to serve. Where would you and I be if the Founding Fathers had left Valley Forge for the comforts of home and family? Or, sadder yet, where would mankind be if Jesus Christ had abandoned his assault on the bureaucracy of the Sanhedrin and the red tape of Judaism? Against today's bureaucracy and red tape the Lord has no voice but ours, and we must place ourselves in a position where the Lord's voice can be heard loud and clear.

When I was eighteen years old I did not come straight to BYU. I went to Glendale Community College. The first day at Glendale was exciting. I lived ten miles from the campus, so my parents let me drive the car to school. By the second day I realized that this wasn't high school anymore. In high school, for example, I had served in student government. There I could walk down the halls and people would recognize me. The sophomores had memorized my name, and people would wave at me. But at Glendale no one cared what student government did, much less who the leaders were.

Three weeks into the school term I went to a Latter-day Saint Student Association conference. At this meeting each of us received a packet of material with an emblem on the outside that said, "The Campus Is Our Cause." I didn't think anything about this until later in the program when speaker after speaker, student body president after student body president, even the two General Authorities who were there, talked about the sacrifice we should be willing to make to give service on our campus. Each speaker said that we should become the light of the gospel at our schools and occupy positions where the Lord's voice could be heard.

I decided to run for student body president. It wasn't for glory. There was no glory in holding this position at Glendale College. There was a regular meeting at seven in the morning I would have to attend. I wasn't excited about that, knowing it would be like waking up for early-morning seminary all over again. But that is what we had to do to make the campus our cause.

I ran for student body president and won. When I was in that position everyone knew that I was a Mormon; I was Carol the Mormon. It was a great missionary opportunity. As a result, a good friend of mine became interested in the Church, and we had many long talks about the gospel. Soon, he was baptized, and he is now attending this university.

Once I was in that position, I had many opportunities to present the Lord's point of view. For example, one day a student came to me and said, "Carol, I have a great idea. My brother goes to Occidental College, and they had a Gay Rights Day there. Why don't we have one here at Glendale? It doesn't have to be anything big. We could just have everyone who sympathizes with gays wear blue jeans to school." This encounter gave me the opportunity to express my views about homosexuality, and as a result Gay Rights Day never became a reality at Glendale College.

We need to be Christ's representatives no matter where we are so that the Lord can look down at us and say, "There is Mary at that meeting; I don't have to worry that my view will not be expressed there." We need what my mother calls intestinal fortitude. We need to have enough courage that no matter where we are we will express the Lord's point of view. City council meetings, school boards, PTA's—all of these are places where the Lord's views need to be presented.

When we hear about becoming involved, informed, and active, most of us say, "That's great, but where do I begin?" Perhaps we can take a lesson from the Nephites, who, when preparing for battle against the Lamanites, first fortified their weakest cities. When the Lamanites came to those places looking for an advantage, they found that those weak places had been made strong.

Where in our communities and in our states do we need to fortify? It might be in the PTA. In my hometown in Glendale, many of the women in the stake are PTA officers and have been making a significant contribution. We might also serve in the city council or on ad hoc committees in community government. When we fortify these places we will have strongholds to work from as we fight other important battles. The Lord has said that he will help us turn our weaknesses into strengths.

While growing up in the Church I found that in almost every youth conference I attended, speakers would tell us that we—the youth of the Church—are a chosen generation. I was even in a singing group that sang, "Oh chosen generation, blessed above all others; ye were sent, ye were meant for such a time as this." That's great, but many young people fail to realize what it takes to become chosen. We are the only ones who can make us chosen. We are free to choose whether we are to be that chosen, blessed generation; it isn't something that we are simply given.

I would like to conclude with the words of the great statesman Patrick Henry, who said, "The battle, sir, is not to the strong alone, but to the vigilant, the active and the brave." May we not only be strong but may we be active, brave, and vigilant in winning the battles we fight against evil in our communities, states, and nation.

Freedom to Become

Mary Frances Sturlaugson

A native of Chattanooga, Tennessee, Mary Frances Sturlaugson is the fifteenth of twenty-four children. She was the first person in her family to graduate from high school, after which she attended Dakota Wesleyan University where she graduated in English. Currently she is pursuing a master's degree in educational psychology at BYU and plans to become a high school guidance counselor.

While attending school in Rosebud, South Dakota, she was contacted by the missionaries and later baptized. A convert of some four years, Sister Sturlaugson was one of the first three blacks, and the first black sister, called on a mission by the Church.

Upon returning from the Texas-San Antonio Mission in March 1980, she authored A Soul So Rebellious, *which recounts her life story.*

In contemplating the subject I would talk about, I reflected over my life prior to my joining the Church. As people have become acquainted with me, there has always seemed to be a common question. I have usually not been confronted with it, but the thoughts have been there. I realized that this was often due to people's feelings of delicacy or their inability to frame the question correctly. Usually I was approached in a half hesitant sort of way, or with eyes of curiosity, or with looks of pity and compassion. But thanks to an honest little fourth grader at Hillcrest Elementary School, the unspoken question was finally posed: "How does it feel to be black?"

This morning I would like to express to you my feelings on how it feels to be black, a female, and a member of The Church of Jesus Christ of Latter-day Saints. The color of my skin has brought me great persecution as well as the most difficult struggle in my life—the struggle of trying to help people understand that this color is god-given, as is any other color. It is not one that was forced on me, but one that I chose to receive.

We often talk and preach about free agency in the premortal existence and in this life. But somehow we seem to fail to comprehend *all* that it means. Or, we comprehend it to a point that is pleasing to us or convenient. Understanding what needed to be accomplished to help each of us return to our Father in Heaven, our brother Jesus Christ said, "Father, send me." Exercising our free agency, each of us also said, "Father, send me." This color—one that has definitely brought about more than its share of persecution and suffering—is the one I chose. Thanks to the beautiful principles of the gospel that were taught to me, I am now able to bear the trials I face because of my color—not with bitterness, but with a heart full of sorrow for those who do not have the understanding of these principles in their lives.

I am sure our Heavenly Father felt great joy and pride as he made the many different colors of flowers, trees, and the other things that beautify this earth. He must have felt even greater pride and joy as he placed his children of all colors upon this earth, but at times we fail to enjoy the beauty of being his children because of differences in skin color. I witness this often as people confront me and ask me what they should call me: "black," "negro," "Afro-American," "colored," or what. When in doubt, I tell them, simply call me "sister." Please do not let the color of my skin keep from you the knowledge of our eternal bond.

Being a female has also brought its share of struggles, and they have been compounded by virtue of my being black. Being a black female seems to bring with it a reputation for having low morals and similar problems, and I am still amazed at how insensitive people can be to the fact that I have feelings and specific goals in mind. Often I meet people who have seen a black man—perhaps down in Moab or some other place—and they seem to automatically feel—no matter what the guy is like—that he and I should get together, simply because of our skin color. Yet we are all taught—black and white—that we should have specific qualities in mind as we look for our eternal mate.

Being a Mormon has given me the greatest comfort I have known as I have faced my trials of being black and female. For to know the will of God is the greatest knowledge, to suffer the will of God is the greatest heroism, to do the will of God is the greatest achievement, and to have the Lord's approval of your work brings the greatest happiness.

Being black, female, and Mormon *is* a struggle. But struggle is the primary law of life. We struggle and we survive. We fail to struggle and we perish. Our salvation is in our own hands, and in the stubbornness of our minds and the tenderness of our hearts. The task is ours. The strength to accomplish that task comes from the true gospel of Jesus Christ. Yes, being black, female, and a member of this Church is a great privilege, but it brings with it a heavy responsibility. My prayer, as I face my trials, is expressed beautifully by Og Mandino in his book, *The Greatest Salesman in the World.* He says:

> Oh creator of all things, help me. For this day I go out into the world naked and alone, and without your hand to guide me I will wander far from the path which leads to success and happiness. I ask not for gold or garments, or even opportunity equal to my ability; instead, guide me so that I may acquire ability equal to my opportunities.... Help me to remain humble through obstacles and

failures; yet hide not from my eyes the prize that will come with victory.... Confront me with fears that will temper my spirit; yet endow me with courage to laugh at my misgivings. Spare me sufficient days to reach my goals; yet help me to live this day as though it be my last. Guide me in my words that they may bear fruit; yet silence me from gossip that none be maligned. Discipline me in the habit of trying and trying again; yet show me the way to make use of the law of averages. Favor me with alertness to recognize opportunity; yet endow me with patience which will concentrate my strength. Bathe me in good habits that the bad ones may drown; yet grant me compassion for weaknesses in others. Suffer me to know that all things shall pass; yet help me to count my blessings of today. Expose me to hate so it not be a stranger; yet fill my cup with love to turn strangers into friends. But all these things be only if thy will. I am a small and lonely grape clutching the vine, yet thou hast made me different from all others. Verily, there must be a special place for me. Guide me. Help me. Show me the way. Let me become all you plan for me when my seed was planted and selected by you to sprout in the vineyard of this world. [New York: Bantam Books, 1974]